The Eucharistic Heart

Jean Galot SJ

VERITAS

Published 1990 by
Veritas Publications
7-8 Lower Abbey Street
Dublin 1

Original French language edition of
Le Coeur Eucharistique
published and copyright 1983 by
Éditions Pierre Tequi
82 Rue Bonaparte
Paris
France

Translation by Sr Áine Hayde
Cover design by Banahan McManus, Dublin
Typesetting by Printset & Design Ltd, Dublin
Printed in the Republic of Ireland by Leinster Leader Ltd., Naas

Contents

Foreword

When I was a student in the seminary during the last war we rose each morning at six o'clock, and after a period of prayer we assembled for Mass. Often sleepy, sometimes cold, we joined in the celebration of the mystery with little more than a spirit of faith to sustain us.

Later I discovered that only a few hundred miles away — we cover the distance today in a couple of hours — there were men and women in the concentration camps of the Third Reich. I have heard it said that on occasion a little wine would be smuggled into the camp and a little bread saved up, that when all was quiet at night they would huddle together, overcoming their fear, and that the priests amongst them would say the words of our Lord to make his sacrifice present amongst them — the oft-repeated story of the Roman catacomb, the Irish Mass rock, the English recusant manor-house, the back room of revolutionary Paris. From the sacrifice of Christ the prisoners drew the strength of the love that kept them going in their sufferings, taught them to love one another, and even to forgive their enemies. 'Do this in memory of me' *(Lk 22:19)*. In following his command they knew that they were not themselves forgotten.

At the time, we knew nothing of all this. And yet, in the security and peace of our seminary chapel, we were drawn into communion with them by that same sacrifice of Christ in his Church, and we grew together with them in the knowledge and love of the Master. By a kind of divine conspiracy our lives had touched in Christ, and I now know that we were the debtors. The mystery of the Eucharist is the mystery in the heart of the Church, the mystery of the communion in the body and blood of the Lord, that unites God's children in the praise of his mercy, as they share together the love made present and active amongst them from the eucharistic heart of Christ.

I am reminded of the inspiring words of Pope John Paul II to the vast throng of the Irish in the homily he preached at Mass in Dublin's Phoenix Park:

> From the upper room in Jerusalem, from the Last Supper, in a certain sense, the Eucharist writes the history of human hearts and of human communities. Let us reflect on all those, who, being nourished on the body and blood of the Lord, have lived and died on this island, bearing in themselves, because of the Eucharist, the pledge of eternal life. Let us think of so many generations of sons and daughters of this country, and at the same time, sons and daughters of the Church. May this Eucharist of ours be celebrated in the atmosphere of the great communion of saints (Homily, Phoenix Park, Dublin, 29 September 1979).

The Second Vatican Council teaches:

> 'The bishop, invested with the fullness of the sacrament of Orders, is 'steward of the grace of the supreme priesthood', above all in the Eucharist, which he himself offers, or ensures that it is offered, from which the Church ever derives its life and on which it thrives... In each altar community, under the sacred ministry of the bishop, a manifest symbol is to be seen of that charity and 'unity of the mystical body, without which there can be no salvation.' In these communities, though they may often be small and poor, or existing in the diaspora, Christ is present through whose power and influence the One, Holy, Catholic and Apostolic Church is constituted. For 'the sharing in the body and blood of Christ has no other effect than to accomplish our transformation into that which we receive' (*Lumen Gentium,* 26).

Because it is the special responsibility of the bishop to celebrate the Eucharist in the midst of his people, he will welcome every initiative that is capable of drawing them into a more faithful participation in this mystery. Contemporary developments in doctrinal and liturgical understanding have brought a renewed and authentic appreciation of the role of the Christian community in the celebration of the Eucharist. The community exists and flourishes only through its union with Christ, the Head of the Body, in so far as he exercises his saving power in such a way as to realise his immediate personal relation with each member. Through the community we are with Christ; through our communion with Christ we live in communion with one another. Because these relations derive their properly personal character from the immediacy of Christ's person, meditation on the eucharistic heart of Christ is a particularly fruitful way to discover the wealth of the Eucharist.

That is why I welcome enthusiastically this work of a great theologian; great not only for his insight and penetration into the treasure of the Church's faith, but for a wisdom that manifests his affinity with the spiritual things of God. Many, especially priests and those formed in theology and in the fervour of a spiritual life, will read it with ease. May they assist many others to discover its wealth and to respond by the grace of Christ to the wonder of his eucharistic heart.

✠ Desmond
Archbishop of Dublin
Feast of Christ the King
26 November 1989

Introduction

If we want to enter into the mystery of the Eucharist, it is not enough to re-read what the gospel accounts and the commentaries of St Paul tell us about the institution of the sacrament. We must try rather to grasp the deep purpose of Jesus and to discover the profound state of mind and heart which led him to bring into being the wonder revealed during the Last Supper.

We must penetrate the secret of his eucharistic heart. All the words and actions of Jesus take their meaning from the underlying attitude which inspires them, an attitude to which they also give expression. They come from his heart. The Eucharist, in a very special way, is the fruit of his heart. And it is not wrong to speak of the eucharistic heart, because the Eucharist holds an important and essential place in the religion established by Christ. Before being instituted, the Eucharist was in the Master's heart; and when it was instituted it showed forth, in a very telling way, Jesus' inner state of mind and heart.

The heart of Christ was a eucharistic heart because the whole of his earthly life was directed towards the gift of himself which he would make in the Eucharist. It also deserves to be called a eucharistic heart because in it we find the fundamental attitude of eucharistic worship, an attitude which had to be transmitted from the Master to the disciples.

We do not speak of the eucharistic heart in order to combine two devotions — devotion to the Sacred Heart and devotion to the Eucharist. Our intention is neither to promote particular devotions nor to unite them, but rather to enter as deeply as possible into the mystery of the Eucharist. It is not possible to examine this mystery without making an effort to discover the heart of Christ which is totally bound up with it.

We would add that when we use the term 'eucharistic heart',

we do not intend to introduce something of a very sentimental nature into our way of looking at the Eucharist. We are trying to grasp how Jesus felt when he instituted the Eucharist. And at the same time we want to get in touch with his will, his purpose and his thought. By the word 'heart' we mean the whole interior being of Christ, his most secret life, his person given in love.

So the eucharistic heart is not some kind of artificial devotion thought up by a few Christians. It is the truth of the Eucharist, its primary meaning as it is revealed to us in the gospels. We will try to discover this mystery in the gospel texts, convinced that we will find it by examining what the evangelists point out to us.

It would be a mistake to think that there is not much to say about the eucharistic heart and that everything has been said in the Church's doctrine on the Eucharist. Every time we explore the gospel texts we discover fascinating traits of Jesus' personality and of his way of thinking, feeling and acting. Indeed, the texts contain an inexhaustible wealth of meaning by the very fact that they were written under the inspiration of the Holy Spirit who placed within them a meaning higher than all human thought. This results in the fact that the study of the gospels places before our eyes a Christ who is always different from the one we imagined, a Christ who is always new.

A study of the eucharistic heart, then, will lead us to new ways of looking at the Lord's heart and at the Eucharist. Of course we already know that this study will show us the basic purpose of Jesus which was one of love. But it is the tangible expressions of this love that we want to try to highlight.

So what we want to understand better is the innermost life of Christ, Christ who lived out the Eucharist himself before handing it over to others. Some of the multiple aspects of this full and overflowing life will emerge to surprise and enrich us. Since it is impossible to take in all the riches of the depths of

Jesus' soul, we will pick out and retain at least some of its characteristic qualities.

We will take St Paul as our guide, first of all in the way in which he sees the effort which Christians must make to get to know the heart of Christ, and then in his account of the institution of the Eucharist where he invites us to go back to discover the Master's interior life. Later we will look more directly at the gospels to see what they show us about the Saviour's eucharistic heart.

1

St Paul's invitation to discover the eucharistic heart

From the time of his meeting with Christ on the road to Damascus, Saul, who became Paul, never ceased to gaze on the One whom he had met. Living in Christ, he tried to get to know, through the tradition of the Christian community and the testimonies of the disciples, the One who had transformed his being. Above all, he wanted to understand what Christ's redemptive work consisted in. With impassioned zeal he spread the knowledge he had acquired about the Saviour and his actions.

Even though his letters do not contain a systematic account of the doctrine of salvation, we find in them an indication of the importance which he attributed to the Eucharist in the Christian life. We also find an invitation to get to know the Christ who loves us.

DISCOVERING THE HEART OF CHRIST

In the epistle to the Ephesians, Paul recalls the grace that he had received 'to preach to the Gentiles the unsearchable riches of Christ and to make all men see what is the plan of the mystery hidden for ages in God'. Then in a prayer addressed to the Father he expresses the desire that all Christians may know these unsearchable riches, and shows at the same time how this knowledge can be developed. May the Father 'according to the riches of his glory grant you to be strengthened with might through his Spirit in the inner man, and that Christ may dwell in your hearts through faith; that you, being rooted and grounded in love, may have power to comprehend with all the saints what is the breadth and length and height and depth, and to know the love of Christ which surpasses knowledge, that you may be filled with all the fullness of God' *(Eph 3:8-9; 16-19)*.

1. Conditions for discovering the heart of Christ
The inner transformation effected by the Father
Knowledge of the love of Christ is not simply the result of a human effort to study Christ. It is even more than the effort to acquire knowledge under the guidance and inspiration of grace. It comes from a whole inner transformation effected in the person by the Father.

First of all, let us be aware that the initiative belongs to the Father. It is the Father who makes his Son known. It is he who sent his Son into the world to reveal God, and it is he, through the Holy Spirit, who enables us to understand this revelation. We remember that, after Jesus had asked his Apostles for a personal profession of faith, and had received Simon's declaration, 'You are the Christ, the Son of the living God', he reacted immediately by affirming that this was not something discovered by human intelligence but was rather a revelation which came from the heavenly Father (Mt 16:16-17). All the clues to his identity which Jesus gave would not have been enough to cause the disciple to make this proclamation in the name of the twelve, a proclamation which was to become the Church's proclamation of faith. Only the Father, through the light which he himself radiates, can enlighten people's minds with the truth about his Son. It was the Father who enabled Peter to see Jesus as he himself saw him, and to put into words the mystery of his person.

In the Letter to the Ephesians, St Paul emphasises the primordial role of the Father by highlighting the strength he gives to Christians. The Father gives not only light but power. 'May he grant you to be strengthened with might through his Spirit', writes the Apostle, because it is through him that Christians receive the power to understand what the love of Christ is. In order to discover the heart of Christ we need spiritual power, the power which the Father gives through the Holy Spirit.

In this way, 'the inner man is strengthened'. Left to themselves, people run the risk of letting themselves become absorbed by everything around them and of living as people who are always turned towards external things, which shape their way of thinking and their inspiration of life. They are in danger of living a superficial life because they have lost the ability to enter into themselves, to reflect and to turn towards the invisible. They become slaves of their senses and of their instinctive reactions. They are carried away by what they actually see and hear. How could these people who are absorbed by what is visible and immediate be interested in Christ and have a desire to discover his heart?

We could say, in Paul's language, that in every human person there is an inner being and an outer being. When the outer being is the only one to be developed, it suffocates the inner being and uses all the individual's energy on surface thoughts and actions. To develop the outer being, all we need to do is let things happen and allow ourselves to be taken up with the multiple attractions of the world around us. But for the development of the inner being we have to make an effort. To combat the obsession with what is visible, we must preserve within ourselves the ability to reflect, to meditate and to be in contact with the invisible. We need to resist being attracted towards what is easy and being seduced by so many things which later on prove to be illusory and of little worth. The inner being too, develops as a result of being attracted and seduced, this time by the interior presence of God. But this attraction and seduction are less obvious and less immediately felt.

The development of the inner being is brought about by the action of the Father who, through the Holy Spirit, forms in the human person an ability to seek and find God. The Spirit comes to 'strengthen' our inner being by giving us the means to overcome all the temptations of the outer world, and by enabling us to triumph over the attractions which make us forget who we are and who we should be.

In strengthening our inner being he creates in us the desire to know Christ and, while getting to know him, not to be satisfied with a superficial approach, which would be confined to accentuating the 'outer Christ', his life as it appeared to his contemporaries. The Spirit enables us to discover above all the 'inner Christ', his deep state of mind and heart, his innermost thoughts, his feelings and intentions. The more the inner being is strengthened in Christians, the more they are able to get to know the inner Christ, and the more they try to discover him in the gospel texts and in their lives.

Going beyond the thought of St Paul, who is not referring directly to the Eucharist in this text, we can note that the building up of the inner being is an effect of the Eucharist. It comes from the Father through the Spirit because the bread of the Eucharist is given by the Father (Jn 6:31) and owes its effectiveness to the Spirit with whom it is filled (Jn 6:63). So the Eucharist itself, by making us more aware of the invisible, makes us more disposed to discover the eucharistic heart of Christ.

The indwelling of Christ in the heart by faith

It may seem paradoxical to state that if we are to discover the heart of Christ, Christ himself must dwell in the heart of Christians by faith. But St Paul realised that we can only penetrate the inner Christ by means of knowledge when we ourselves have already been penetrated interiorly by Christ. Paul himself was aware that Christ lived in him. 'It is no longer I who live, but Christ who lives in me; and the life I now live in the flesh I live by faith in the Son of God, who loved me and gave himself for me' *(Gal 2:20)*. This personal witness shows how the life of Christ, which developed in him because of his faith, enabled him to understand how much the Son of God loved him. He wanted all Christians to have the same experience and he asked the Father to make Christ dwell in their hearts by faith so that they would know the love of Christ.

When the Father sent his Son into the world he wanted him to live on earth as a human being. St John, writing of the Incarnation, says, 'The Word became flesh and dwelt among us' *(Jn 1:14)*. He could dwell among us only if he became a human being. By becoming flesh the Word was able to live like other people. And that is what seems to be the important thing about the Incarnation — his desire to live a life like ours. By dwelling among us, the Son of God really became part of our world and of human society. He stayed with us, he lived in our company.

However, his 'dwelling among us' was fragile and transitory like every human life. When the evangelist says 'he dwelt' he uses a verb which calls to mind the nomads who lived under a tent.[1] In the divine plan, the transient dwelling of Jesus among us was the prelude to another more permanent kind of dwelling.

Jesus moved from dwelling among us in an external way to an interior dwelling within our hearts. When he left this earth to enter into heavenly glory, he wanted to be part of the life of the human race in a more profound way than he had been during his time on earth. He becomes present to those who open themselves to him by faith, to the point of abiding habitually in the inner space which they give him.

He promised those who love him and keep his command-

---

1. *Eskenosen* resembles *skene,* a tent. 'A lovely biblical expression to describe the nomadic life', says M.J. Lagrange. (*Evangile selon Saint Jean,* Paris, 1925, 20)

ments, that he and his Father would come and dwell in them. 'If a man loves me, he will keep my word and my Father will love him, and we will come to him and make our home with him' *(Jn 14:23)*. Here Jesus emphasises that the initiative comes from the Father. It is because of his love that the Father comes to us at the same time as his Son.

Those who have Christ dwelling in their hearts are better able to discern the greatness of his love. By moving from an external to an interior way of dwelling among us, Christ helped to make the inner being prevail over the outer being. He encouraged people to look for what was hidden deep behind appearances. While Jesus lived on earth people could be content to look at his outer appearance and to see him with human eyes. When he came to dwell within their hearts, they were invited to seek the inner Christ, the One who by his love satisfies the deepest yearnings of the human heart. They became more aware of the incompleteness of a superficial knowledge of Jesus' words and actions.

The deep relationships which Christ establishes with those in whom he comes to dwell lead them to try to penetrate the most secret places in the Saviour's soul. The One who dwells in their hearts poses the problem of his identity from within, 'Who do you say that I am?' *(Mk 8:29)*. And he awaits a response which tries to express the richness of his personality and heart, and not one which just gives him a name.

Once again we can note that the indwelling of Christ is strengthened by the Eucharist. In communion, Christ comes to give his sacramental presence to Christians and enables them to be more vividly aware of the mystery of his habitual presence in them. That is why sharing in the eucharistic meal impels Christians to try to know the One whose presence they receive. In the intimacy of communion they hear a voice saying, 'Who do you say that I am?' and are spurred on to discover the Lord and his eucharistic heart.

Rooted in love

In wishing that Christians be 'rooted and grounded in love', St Paul is visualising at the root of their behaviour, a very deep charity on which their spiritual life would be built.

He is not recommending the practice of charity only; he wants to ensure that the principle of charity is there. The practice of charity implies an effort to observe all that is required by the double commandment to love both God and our neighbour. It has very far-reaching implications because the love of God must be expressed in multiple attitudes of faith, trust, adoration, praise, offering and thanksgiving. Love of our neighbour has a wide variety of practical applications, none of which can be neglected: kindness in thought and word, respect, friendliness, acceptance, patience, service, understanding and forgiveness of mistakes, mutual aid in helping the poor and unfortunate, the thousand ways of being attentive to others. The practice of charity consists also in the struggle against showing selfishness and pride, against inclinations to jealousy, against instincts of violence and aggression, against resentment and the desire for revenge, against rash judgement, against withdrawal into mistrust and suspicion, against the tendency to anger, intolerance and hurtful words, against hardness of heart. On other occasions, St Paul mentions some of these practical demands. In the same letter to the Ephesians he writes, 'Let all bitterness and wrath and anger and clamour and slander be put away from you, with all malice, and be kind to one another, tenderhearted, forgiving one another, as God in Christ forgave you' *(Eph 4:31-32)*.

The practice of charity in its multiple forms should be the result of a rootedness in love. The Apostle wants to draw our attention to the need to interiorise charity just as he emphasised his desire that the inner being be built up. Love must be at the source of all behaviour. It must be an inner strength which prompts numerous exterior acts of charity. The depths of our soul must be bathed in love if our efforts to love God and our neighbour in a practical way are not to be artificial, but rather the result of an overflowing of the depths of our being seeking to express itself.

In asking Christians not to grieve the Holy Spirit in whom they were sealed (Eph 4:30), Paul makes them understand how rootedness in love comes about. The Holy Spirit who in his very person is divine love, comes to pour the love of God into our hearts (Rm 5:5). It is he who ensures that the love of God does not remain outside human persons, but enters into them. He forms in them a divine source of love which enables them to keep the commandment of charity, and love as God loves. So it is the Holy Spirit who brings about the interiorisation of love by placing love at the root of all the individual's activities.

He enables the human person to pour out such generous love that it reflects the love of God and Christ. 'Therefore be imitators of God, as beloved children. And walk in love, as Christ loved us and gave himself up for us' *(Eph 5:1-2)*. Actually, Christians should love one another as Christ loved them. They should make their own the Saviour's state of mind and heart, which he showed in the supreme act of his sacrifice. 'Have this mind among yourselves, which is yours in Christ Jesus', Paul says somewhere else in placing before the eyes of the Christians the heroism of their Saviour in his self-emptying and sacrifice (Phil 2:5). He exhorts them in the name of the urgent call of Christ and 'communion in the Spirit' to maintain unity: 'Complete my joy by being of the same mind, having the same love, being in full accord and of one mind. Do nothing from selfishness or conceit, but in humility, count others better than yourselves. Let each of you look not only to his own interests, but also to the interests of others' *(Phil 2:2-4)*. This kind of behaviour is ensured by conformity to the deep state of mind and heart of Christ, and it is the Holy Spirit who brings about this conformity, by penetrating the heart of his disciples with the love of the Master.

Being rooted in love then means that through the Holy Spirit we receive in ourselves a strength to love which is like Christ's power to love. We must bear this likeness within ourselves in order to get to know the heart of Christ. It is by being invaded to the depths of our soul by the love of Jesus that we become able to understand this love. It is a question of a knowledge which comes forth from within the person. The more the depths of the human person are taken over by love, the more his or her mind will be able to grasp the secret depth of Christ's love.

Once again we should note that this way of looking at things is particularly suited to the Eucharist even though that is not what Paul is referring to. The Eucharist has always been considered a sacrament of unity and charity. It reproduces the sacrifice which brought about the reconciliation of the human race, and in the communion meal it transmits to Christians the higher power to love which belongs to the Lord. By nourishing Christians with the body of Christ it roots them in love by making Christ's life of love overflow into them. It grounds them in love by giving them an unshakeable support in the building up of a life of giving and offering. And in this way it enables them to discover the eucharistic heart of the Lord. By nourishing their spiritual life with the very life of Christ it fills them with love to the full; thanks to this intimate penetration it enables them to understand the immensity of the love into which they are plunged.

2. Knowing the love of Christ

Knowing the love which surpasses knowledge
Paul affirms the unique worth of knowing the love of Christ; it means knowing something which surpasses all knowledge. It is the highest possible knowledge that the human mind can aim to achieve. To know the love of Christ means to go beyond all other kinds of knowledge.

It means that human intelligence reaches the ultimate goal of its thirst for knowledge. In actual fact what it desires to know above all is God. In Christ, God takes on a human face, he speaks a human language and does human things. By living in the midst of people Christ revealed to them the face of God which, according to Jewish tradition, was impossible to see. He didn't hesitate to say to the disciple who asked him to show him the Father, 'He who has seen me has seen the Father' (Jn 14:9). He offered to those around him the possibility of seeing God with their eyes of flesh.

By giving them the possibility of seeing God, he allowed them to get to know what is deepest within him, his love. If the human mind aspires to know God above all things, its desire is to explore the very depths of God, to go as far as possible in penetrating the mystery of his divinity. The supreme victory of human intelligence, made possible by the revelation of Christ, is to understand the truth proclaimed by St John, 'God is love' (1 Jn 4:8).

However, Paul does not just say that the knowledge of the love of Christ surpasses all other kinds of knowledge. He states that it really surpasses *all* knowledge. We could be tempted to see a contradiction here. If the love of Christ really surpasses all knowledge, how is it that we can still truly get to know him? In fact Paul shows us quite clearly what he means; to know the love of Christ surpasses all human knowledge. Prayer addressed to the Father shows us that we are touching on something divine. It is the Father who, by strengthening our inner being through the Holy Spirit and rooting it in love, enables us to know what is beyond the reach of human intelligence.

It would be useless, therefore, to want to get to know the love of Christ by human power. It sometimes happens that we want to approach the gospel as we approach an account of the life of a great person, or that we try to imagine Jesus in the way we would try to imagine a person like ourselves. We want to bring him closer to everyone by attributing to him a personality like our own. We tend to see in him a reflection of what we ourselves are. Some have seen in him the person of their dreams; the benefactor of society, the friend who tolerates and approves of everything, the reformer in solidarity with the unfortunate, the revolutionary who advocates a revolt against injustice, the idealist who has come to free us from the pressures of an over-complicated social life and to open the way of simplicity for us.

There are various human reconstructions of the person of Jesus which do not correspond exactly to the truth, precisely because they are too human in the sense that they turn Jesus into a human ideal, which we invent to suit ourselves. They are based on a reading of the gospels which is too human, or on an interpretation dictated by opinions which also are too human.

In order to know Christ, we must accept the fact that we cannot get to know him by a simple effort of human intelligence. We must be open to the revelation from above which comes from the Father and allow ourselves to be guided by the Holy Spirit in our reading of the gospel texts. Instead of giving Christ the face that we would like him to have, we must receive as a heavenly gift the face which is depicted for us in the gospels. The face of the Son of God made man should be received as it is, unique and always surprising.

In order to know the love of Christ we must accept that this love is different from our concepts of love, which are too skimpy, and that we need a higher light if we are to enter into the revelation of this exceptional love. The more we get to know this love, the more we should feel that it is beyond us and recognise that it is greater than we could ever imagine. The moment we think that we know what this love is like and that we can express it adequately, it is no longer the real authentic love, because the love of Christ surpasses all knowledge. What we discover of the heart of Christ will never be more than a glimpse of what we are searching for.

Understanding the dimensions of the world
Paul hopes that Christians will be able 'to comprehend what is the breadth and length and height and depth'. Sometimes people have wanted to apply these dimensions to the love of

Christ; some have even tried to explain what the breadth, length, height and depth of this love consisted in. But that is not the meaning of the text. Paul speaks of these dimensions in an absolute way; he does not qualify them. He is using the language of the philosophers of his time, especially of the Stoics, who considered that the supreme aim of science was to know the dimensions of the world.[2] Understanding the breadth, length, height and depth meant having a commanding vision of all the contours of the universe and consequently knowing everything about it; it meant bringing it entirely within the scope of knowledge. Those who succeeded in understanding the absolute dimensions of the universe would find themselves in possession of all the secrets of the world.

And so Paul's idea becomes clearer: if we want to understand the dimensions of the world we must know the love of Christ. When we know this love we understand the meaning of length, breadth, height and depth. The secret of the universe is hidden in the heart of Christ. When we discover his heart we know all things.

So here we have a fruitful way of looking at what knowledge of the love of Christ brings. We might have thought that this knowledge would be of interest only for understanding Jesus' feelings for a psychological study. But now we see that it sheds light over the whole world. It does even more, because by obtaining the secret of all things, the discovery of the heart of Christ enlightens all other kinds of knowledge. It transforms people's way of looking at the world around them.

The love of Christ is the enlightening principle of the global destiny of the universe and of everything within the universe. Paul affirms that everything will find its final meaning in Christ when he speaks of the Father's plan to 'unite' all things in Christ, things in heaven and things on earth (Eph 1:10). Everything is destined to be restored and unified in Christ and placed under

---

2. Cf J. Dupont, *Gnosis,* Louvain, 1949, 476 ff.

his dominion. At the centre of this plan, we find the love of the Father, which is manifested to us in the love of the Saviour, in whom we have redemption with all the riches of divine grace (Eph 1:5-7).

Therefore the love of Christ contains the secret of the whole history of the universe as it is accomplished according to the divine plan. It is what gives meaning to the physical evolution of the universe and of life, and also to the moral and spiritual development of the human race; because everything was created in view of the coming and spreading of this love, and it was this love which, through the Sacrifice, saved the human community by raising it to the level of a new creation more wonderful than the first.

Paul was not wrong to list all the possible dimensions in order to affirm that once we know the love of God we understand them all. The multiple aspects of all that is real, as well as all the things which mark the life of the human race should be interpreted on the basis of this love. To be more exact, it is in this love that we understand the purpose which leads the universe towards its final end. It gives an explanation of history from within through the hidden power which is unfolded throughout the whole exterior mosaic of events.

It must be emphasised that this explanation does not remain in the domain of theory. It gives people a very tangible meaning to their existence.

Let us take the example of suffering. We know how bewildering trials may be for the human mind and what agonising questions they pose for the afflicted heart. All the sufferings which overwhelm people's personal lives can be explained in the final analysis by the love of Christ. It is in the light of this love that we see the true place of human suffering. All trials are destined to unite us to the work of redemption which is the essential work of the love of Christ. Because Christ loved to the end, we are invited to love like he did, through trials similar to his.

Knowing the love of Christ means understanding the dimension of suffering and of all the other real situations which make up human existence. This knowledge enables us to interpret authentically all that passes before our eyes, to give everything a deeply optimistic interpretation in keeping with the loving kindness of the divine plan.

Entering into the fullness of God
When we know the love of Christ we are ready to receive the divine fullness and to enter into the pleroma, i.e. the formation of a universe where the fullness of God reigns.

What has already been said about discovering the heart of Christ is sufficient evidence that the knowledge referred to is more than intellectual knowledge. Knowledge is the result of a life totally permeated by the presence of Christ and his love.

Knowing means experiencing a love with which we are already impregnated. Through this experience we are open to the divine fullness which Christ brought to the human race. There is a rapturous expansion of the whole being, a new capacity is given to human powers.

We can only discover the heart of Christ by experiencing a release deep within ourselves and feeling carried along by the fullness of the love which we discover. Here, we are far from the kinds of discovery which imply only the cold perception of certain facts. The love of Christ is revealed only with a warmth which is its own and it is revealed to those who allow themselves to be won over by this warmth. In showing itself in this way it gives us an appreciation of the fullness of God manifested in it. Every individual is filled with a love which is the love of God.

If knowledge of the love of Christ overflows from a life rooted in this love, we must not be led to the conclusion that it is useless to examine the gospel texts in order to understand the Master's state of mind and heart. When Paul was writing his letters, the gospels had not yet been composed. But, in order to know Christ, the one who had been converted on the road to

Damascus was not content with the contact he had at that privileged moment. He went to the disciples to get information about who Jesus was and about what he said and did. And it was on the basis of this evidence, and with the experience of a life filled with his presence, that he developed his knowledge of the Saviour.

We always need to go back to the testimonies of the gospels to develop and deepen our knowledge of Christ. The experience which we have of his presence in us is not enough. It prepares us to understand the meaning of the gospel texts more clearly. It is by means of these texts that we discover the master's heart, the multiple signs of his love. There is always something new in the discovery we make through a careful study of what was written under the inspiration of the Spirit. Christians are never dispensed from coming back to the text; they can never think that they have read the gospels enough. This reading is an unlimited undertaking which never ends. The task of discovery has no boundaries, because the love of Christ has none.

An ever-wider and ever-deeper knowledge of the love of Christ must nourish the fullness of divine life. The end of Paul's prayer for Christians remains significant. To know the love of Christ, which surpasses all knowledge, is a very high aim. But it is not the ultimate objective. Knowledge is meant to foster a more abundant life.

The love of Christ shows God's intention to give himself totally to the human race; this is the gift which we are asked to receive. We receive it by making an effort to know, but also by an opening of our whole soul. We must allow ourselves to be penetrated by a love in which the fullness of the truth and life of God is communicated to us.

It is useful to emphasise that in this way of looking at the Eucharist, the link between the knowledge of the love of Christ and the fullness of God is more obvious; the eucharistic food which reveals the intensity of the Lord's love brings a fullness of the divine gift.

DISCOVERING THE EUCHARISTIC HEART

In certain words of St Paul we can discern an invitation to discover the eucharistic heart of Christ.

1. 'I received from the Lord'

When he wants to remind the Corinthians about the true meaning of the Eucharist by referring back to its institution by the Lord, the Apostle writes: 'For I received from the Lord what I also delivered to you, that the Lord Jesus on the night he was betrayed took bread, and when he had given thanks he broke it, and said, "This is my body which is for you. Do this in remembrance of me." In the same way also the cup, after supper, saying, "This cup is the new covenant in my blood. Do this, as often as you drink it, in remembrance of me" ' *(1 Co 11:23-25)*.

The most essential words used by Paul as a guarantee of the value of his account are, 'I received from the Lord'. What do they mean? Commentators of former times thought that St Paul was claiming to have received an exceptional revelation from Christ. Some modern exegetes, notably certain Protestants who considered Paul to have created the Eucharist, have also interpreted this primordial statement to mean that he had a personal vision. But, even grammatically, the expression used by Paul suggests that he is referring to a truth received by means of a tradition going back to the Lord. The Lord is given as the primary origin rather than the immediate source of transmission.[3]

In stating 'I received from the Lord what I also delivered to you', Paul wants to emphasise that far from claiming a personal privilege of revelation or vision in this matter, he only handed over what he had received through the teaching given in the

---

3. The preposition used is *apo*. As J. Jeremias observes, '1 Co 11:23 affirms only one thing: the chain of tradition goes back to the words of Jesus himself without any interruption'. (*La Dernière Cène. Les Paroles de Jésus*, Paris, 1972, 113)

Church. The verbs used for 'to receive' and 'to deliver' correspond to those which in the Jewish language were used with reference to the conservation of tradition.[4] Paul says that he was only a link in the faithful handing on of tradition. What he taught the Corinthians was not his own interpretation or opinion, but only the account guaranteed by tradition.

However, when he refers to tradition, he does not hesitate to give the Lord as its primary origin. It is from Christ that the whole mystery of the Eucharist flows.

We see the true value of this mentioning of the Lord when the text is compared with the other one in the same Letter to the Corinthians which makes explicit appeal to tradition: 'For I delivered to you as of first importance what I also received, that Christ died for our sins in accordance with the scriptures, that he was buried, that he was raised on the third day in accordance with the scriptures ...' *(1 Co 15:3-4)*. The tradition which St Paul relates deals with the foundation of the Christian religion, the work of salvation which is accomplished through the death and resurrection of Christ. It is significant that, in his letter, Paul twice refers expressly to the tradition of the community — once when he makes a statement about Christ's redemptive death and resurrection, and again when he speaks about the institution of the eucharistic meal. In this way he shows the value which he attaches to the Eucharist: on the cultural level its importance is on a parallel with the importance of the paschal mystery in the order of the historical events which ensured our salvation. The Eucharist belongs to the essence of Christianity.

To guarantee the truth of the resurrection, he is content to say, 'what I myself received'. For the Eucharist he says more: 'I received from the Lord'. At the origin of the first tradition we find the witnesses of the resurrection, the women and the apostles who had seen the risen Christ with their own eyes. At

4. cf. Jeremias, ibid.

the origin of the tradition of the Eucharist we have the desire manifested by Christ, his purpose which was expressed in the gestures and words of the Last Supper. So, in order to understand the meaning of eucharistic worship, we must refer back to the eucharistic heart of Christ.

2. 'Do this in memory of me.'

Along with the desire to refer back to the Lord, goes Paul's concern to mention the order to repeat the consecration both of the bread and of the wine. 'Do this in memory of me.'[5] He wants to highlight the express desire of Jesus. If the only things Christians have retained of the paschal meal are the two consecrations, it is because of this desire of the Master, who prescribed the rite which was to be celebrated. If there had not been the double order to do this again, the disciples could have taken the whole Last Supper meal as a eucharistic practice. But they fulfilled Christ's purpose by limiting themselves to the words said over the bread and cup. They left aside all the other rites of the Jewish Passover.

A new meal

They understood especially the Lord's desire to institute a new meal, which would not be something exceptional like the paschal meal, and for which there would be no need to sacrifice a lamb. While the paschal meal was eaten only once a year, Jesus, by prescribing no more than the repetition of the consecration of the bread and cup, shows that his purpose was to institute an ordinary, normal meal, which would be suitable for nourishing the everyday life of his disciples. The first Christians understood and accepted the Master's purpose faithfully, because the breaking of bread was celebrated in their homes every day (Acts 2:46). The frequency of the eucharistic meal responded, in the order of the spiritual life, to that of material meals. In order

---

5. 1 Co 11:24-25. Luke reserved this order for the consecration of the bread (22:19).

to live we must eat every day. The ideal of daily participation in the Eucharist is touched on in a veiled and implicit way in the statements in which Jesus presents his flesh as real food and his blood as real drink: 'Truly, truly I say to you, unless you eat the flesh of the Son of man and drink his blood, you have no life in you' *(Jn 6:53)*. Eucharistic food is as necessary for nourishing life as the daily meal is for physical life. It will fulfil this function as long as the eucharistic meal is taken daily.

In the desire of Christ to become food and drink for the daily life of Christians, we can see the love by which he wants to place himself entirely at our disposal, with all the life that he possesses. He even takes the risk of this meal becoming banal. If he had instituted a meal reserved to a single feast-day each year, he would, by that fact alone, have drawn attention to what an extraordinary favour it is to participate in the Eucharist. By giving himself as daily food and drink, he accepts in advance the danger of routine and habit which will prevent some people from fully appreciating the gift given to them, and from receiving it with the wonder and gratitude it deserves.

Jesus plumbs the depths of the love which dictated the institution of the meal. He places no limits on its frequency and he shows that the Eucharist is the ordinary condition of Christian life, destined therefore to be daily as far as possible. He desires that the efficacy of the gift of his body and blood be as great as possible and that those whom he wants to nourish will continually draw from it the strength that they need.

The sign of bread is characteristically meaningful in this regard. There is no food more ordinary than bread. It is the food of every day. And Jesus himself, in the prayer which he teaches his disciples, recommends them to ask the Father for their daily bread. By 'daily bread' he means material bread, but even more so spiritual bread, because all the petitions of the Our Father — even those which are most directly concerned with our well-being — have a spiritual thrust. So he encourages Christians to ask for eucharistic bread for each day. The Father who feeds his children and gives them the true bread from heaven (Jn 6:32), is prepared to get them their most essential food, the body of his own Son, each day.

The intention of ensuring the daily celebration of the Eucharist in the Church reveals a special characteristic of the eucharistic heart of Jesus: the desire to give himself to the maximum in order to fulfil to the maximum the spiritual needs of the human race. This desire is manifested in his relationship as Son to the Father. Since it is the Father who gives daily bread, Jesus wants to be the daily bread *par excellence*. In giving his Son, the Father wanted to give everything. The Son, in giving himself as daily food, highlights the Father's gift, the summit of divine generosity.

Memory and memorial
No less significant for the revelation of the eucharistic heart is the expression 'Do this in memory of me.'

Jesus did not want his memory to disappear from our spirits. We perceive the implications of this desire at the moment when his body is about to disappear from the sight of those who have known him. He gives his disciples the mission of remembering him.

In their desire to live on, human beings look for something that can perpetuate their memory and ensure them a certain immortality on earth. Ambition, selfishness and pride can play a part in this.

Where Jesus is concerned, the words 'Do this in memory of me' are not inspired by any attachment to himself. They are for the good of all those who want to have this remembrance.

We cannot forget that by these words he places himself boldly at the centre of the new type of worship. The paschal meal was celebrated in memory of Yahweh, who had delivered his people from the Egyptian yoke. The new Passover must be celebrated in memory of Jesus. The 'Me' whom we must remember is the 'Me' of One who is God and who, as such, can demand that thought, prayer and adoration be concentrated on himself.

The 'Me' of Jesus, being a divine 'Me', has the authority to demand that he be remembered by the human race. But he is not trying to oblige people to remember him. He wants the action done in memory of him to be the fruit of love. The order to repeat what he did is given to the disciples whom he called to follow him, whom he called his friends and to whom he wished to communicate his priesthood. From them he has the right to expect the upsurge of love which will lead them to remember him and to rejoice in the remembrance. His eucharistic heart desires that all celebrations carried out in memory of him be carried out through a love which is a response to his love.

The words 'Do this in memory of me' should re-echo in every celebration as the stirring remembrance of those who keep before their eyes the picture of Jesus as he appears in the gospels. They should express the sentiments of those who turn towards the 'Me' of the Lord as the centre of their lives. They will bear witness to the fascination which this 'Me' exercises over people of all times. They should also proclaim repeatedly and forever the love with which the Saviour wishes to gather the whole human race around his person.

It must be added, however, that these words do not envisage simply a subjective remembering by those who are celebrating the Eucharist. Their aim is to bring about objectively the memory of Jesus by the eucharistic act itself. Sometimes they have been translated as, 'Do this as my memorial.'[6] A memorial has a more objective consistency than a simple memory. In the Book of Exodus God, when speaking of the day of the Passover when the people knew that they would be delivered, said, 'This day shall be for you a memorial day, and you shall keep it as a feast to the Lord' *(Ex 12:14)*. The aim of this was to have this day remembered continually. '... that

6. *'Do this as my memorial'* is the title of a work by F. Chenderlin, Rome, 1982.

all the days of your life you may remember the day when you came out of the land of Egypt' *(Dt 16:3)*. This subjective memory, which was to last, was expressed in an objective memory — a memorial — by the feast of the Passover and the meal of the paschal lamb.

The objective character of memory is accentuated in the Eucharist instituted by Jesus. The memorial consists not only in the solemnity of a meal, but in a liturgical act, which results in the presence of his body and blood so that the memory of the Lord becomes his real presence. This happens not because of psychological force or the intensity of the memory, but because of the power of the 'Me' of Christ, who acts through the words of the celebrant. It is the Lord who makes himself present. However, in order to do this he needs to have words said in his name, in memory of him. The celebrant's subjective memory is therefore the means by which the memorial becomes something fully real.

The fact that the memorial is objectively something real helps us to understand better that Christ's purpose was inspired by love alone. Jesus does not want to be remembered after his death for his own personal satisfaction. What he wants is to be able to give himself as food and drink by means of this remembrance. It is a remembrance which he abandons to the human race in such a way that people may be satiated with it. In transforming this remembrance into presence he wants to hand it over to them and make it part of their innermost lives.

It remains true that his eucharistic heart claims a central place in the thought and lives of all. The Eucharist can only be celebrated in the perspective defined by the words 'in memory of me'. It cannot be a simple friendly meal of Christians gathered together to celebrate their charity. It is, above all, the remembrance of Christ, and a remembrance which is so captivating that it dominates the meal and gives it its consistency. In the Eucharist, as in Christian life, the 'Me' of Christ takes priority over the 'me' of Christians. It is he who gathers them together and who binds them more closely to one another by giving them his body as food.

In the Eucharist the prophetic word of Jesus is fulfilled in a more special way — 'And I, when I am lifted up from the earth, will draw all men to myself' *(Jn 12:32)*. The greatest act of Christian worship is the one where we allow ourselves to be drawn by Christ and repeat in his memory what he did at the Last Supper.

However, it must be said again: Christ wants to draw all people to himself only to ensure their destiny and secure their happiness. The words 'in memory of me' are not the words of a selfish person who sets himself as the centre of all the others, but they are the words of a loving person, who wants to give himself to all and share the highest kind of life with them. The eucharistic heart focuses attention on itself only because it is the heart of a God who wants to gather all people in himself.

'On the night he was betrayed'
In Paul's account, pointing out that the time was 'on the night he was betrayed' gives a value of poignancy to Jesus' gesture. It gives us an idea of the emotion with which the Lord instituted the meal of his body and blood, and in this way brings us more expressly into the mystery of his eucharistic heart.

It helps us to discover the indissoluble link which joins sacrifice and meal in the Eucharist. It was instituted when the Sacrifice was imminent. Jesus knew that he had already been drawn into the drama in which he was going to lose his life. It was by committing himself in the sacrificial offering that he was going to give himself as food to his disciples.

It was a solemn moment in the earthly life of Jesus. It was the last time he was still free to act as he wished. After the Last Supper would come the arrest, the trial and the agony. Jesus made final arrangements to ensure the future of the community which he had founded. The Eucharist expresses the last wish of the One about to die. It is also his supreme gift. The eucharistic heart of the Saviour is the last state of his heart before his passion and death.

Mention of the night is evocative. John the evangelist notes that when Judas went out, 'it was night' *(Jn 13:30)*. And according to Luke, Jesus, when he was being arrested, declared to his adversaries: 'But this is your hour, and the power of darkness' *(Lk 22:53)*. The night into which Judas was plunged was the night of betrayal. And this betrayal was carried out during the Last Supper.

At the moment when he wanted to give himself in the Eucharist, the heart of Christ was experiencing the suffering of seeing himself betrayed. Already, before the event, it was from the eucharistic heart that the words broke out, 'Did I not choose you, the twelve, and one of you is a devil?' *(Jn 6:70)*. Jesus had just promised the Eucharist, and he had asked the twelve for loyalty in faith by asking them either to believe or to go away. Judas remained, but without believing. In this disciple the betrayal had begun to take shape in relation to the Eucharist.

At the Last Supper Jesus showed himself to be deeply moved when he announced the betrayal which was now imminent. 'He was troubled in spirit and testified, "Truly, truly, I say to you, one of you will betray me" ' *(Jn 13:21)*. He said it as something almost unbelievable, but at the same time undeniably true. The disciples themselves were thrown into confusion and asked each other who it could be.

From the details given to us in the Fourth Gospel we can see a contrast between the attitude of John the beloved disciple and that of Judas. John was right beside Jesus at the eucharistic table and it was when he had his head laid on Jesus' breast that he asked him who was going to betray him. Later on, John would be called the disciple who had lain close to the Lord's breast (Jn 21:20).

This unique and privileged moment of intimacy with Christ would continue in one way or another to mark his whole life. It is the moment of the Eucharist. The Master had always shown a special affection for John, but it was at the Last Supper that the heart of the Master was opened even more to the disciple. John, who knew the heart of Jesus by experience, realised in the deepest intimacy during the Last Supper what his eucharistic heart was. He is the exemplar of those who, through the Eucharist, discover the most intense joy of intimacy with Christ and who will seek, in this way, to lie close to the Lord's breast.

The presence of Judas did not inhibit the generosity of the eucharistic heart. Even though he was upset by the disciple's dark plan, Jesus did not reject him. He gave him his piece of bread in a gesture of communion, which Judas would not have accepted if he were not going to give up his plan. And since Judas persisted in his intentions, he tried to turn him away from them by showing him that he knew his true feelings: 'What you are going to do, do quickly' *(Jn 13:27)*. He expressly chose to use veiled language which the other disciples would not understand, but whose meaning Judas would grasp. He wanted to invite him quietly to conversion.

The attitude which he adopted towards Judas shows that the eucharistic heart of Christ remains essentially open even to those who are closed. Judas obstinately and ever more firmly closes himself from the Master and his saving love. Jesus opens himself to him; the offer of eucharistic communion is presented to him just as it is to the others. Perhaps Judas had communicated intimately with Christ before receiving the piece of bread. The Master suffered the perverse dispositions of his disciple, just as his heart would later suffer those who approach the Eucharist with a bad conscience. But he does not withhold anything of his eucharistic availability.

If he did not allow himself to be discouraged by the betrayal which had already begun, it was in order to carry out the work of the Father, who would make use of this betrayal to achieve his objective. 'To be handed over' does not just mean being handed over to adversaries by a traitor, it also means being handed over to the redemptive sacrifice by the Father. The night

Jesus was betrayed was the night on which the Father led him on to the road to Calvary.

His intimate relationship with the Father was the most fundamental characteristic of his eucharistic heart. Handed over by the Father to the passion and death, he wanted to go right to the end of the way marked out for him. Since the Father had committed him on the path of total gift in sacrifice, he wanted to hand himself over in the Eucharist, because this would enable him to extend this total gift in history, and place it at the disposal of all. The institution of the Eucharist is explained by Jesus' desire as Son to respond to the primordial purpose of the Father, who handed him over.

2

The great desire

St Luke has left us a record of the first words which Jesus said when he came to table with his apostles for the Last Supper. 'I have earnestly desired to eat this passover with you before I suffer' *(Lk 22:15)*.

'I HAVE EARNESTLY DESIRED'

1. A unique desire

The Hebrew way of expressing an intense desire is to say, 'I have desired with desire'. The repetition of the word 'desire' indicates a strong desire. Translations try to express this intensity by saying, 'I have earnestly desired', or 'I have desired so much'. The Hebrew expression is stronger still. We could comment on it by saying that it is a desire which is pure desire, or a desire which is desire and nothing else. It is desire *par excellence*, a desire which captures the whole of our heart.

This is the only gospel text in which we find the expression. Jesus had never manifested such a desire in any other confidence he gave to his disciples. It is therefore something unique. From what we can deduce from the gospel witness, there had never before been such a desire and there would never again be such a strong one during the earthly life of the Saviour.

We can observe too that the gospels rarely report what Jesus says concerning his personal desires with regard to his life or destiny. The Master does not display his own desires. He speaks rather of the mission entrusted to him by the Father; how he came, not to be served, but to serve. Above all, he makes sure that he is available, and thinks of the desires and needs of others rather than of himself. He says little about his tastes and hopes. If he expresses his desire at the beginning of the paschal meal it is because he wants to make sure that the disciples understand the importance of what he is going to do. He reveals this desire in order to instruct them and not simply for his personal satisfaction. This desire is part of the mystery of the institution of the Eucharist. The disciples must have remembered it as the unforgettable beginning of that institution.

It is a desire which Jesus expressed the night before he died. If it is intense it is because the Saviour has come to the end of his life and because the Eucharist appears as the crown of his work. The paschal meal, which is about to begin, is the climax of the life which he led with his apostles.

Luke is careful to say, 'When the hour came, he sat at table and the apostles with him'. Jesus had often eaten with his disciples, but the hour of this meal was an exceptional one. It was the long awaited hour when his desire could be realised.

Like all the hours in Jesus' life, it had been fixed by the divine plan. During the whole of his earthly life, Jesus fulfilled the mission entrusted to him by the Father. The reason that the intensity of the desire did not turn into impatience to bring forward the time of the meal was that this hour had been decided by the One who governed his life.

So while he was seating himself at table surrounded by his disciples, he knew that he was carrying out the sovereign will of the Father. He inaugurated this meal with a fully committed heart — the heart of a Son. As well as that, the certainty that he was carrying out the Father's plan strengthened his desire. When he declared, 'I have earnestly desired', he was aware that he was expressing a desire which corresponded to the supreme desire of the Father. The Father was the first to have desired the meal where the Eucharist would be instituted. Jesus was, in effect, the living revelation of the Father. The unique desire which captured his whole soul revealed the unique desire of the Father who, if he had spoken in a human language would have said: 'I have earnestly desired'. For the Father, it was a divine and eternal desire. For Jesus, the desire was human. It was the desire of the Son, who had taken the Father's desire and made it his own, while at the same time being the desire of a man who saw that death was close and who wanted to end his life and mission with something beautiful.

2. The desire for the work of redemption and the desire for the Eucharist

Previously, during his public life and in unknown circumstances, Jesus had expressed another intense desire: 'I have come to cast fire upon the earth; and would that it were already kindled! I have a baptism to be baptised with; and how I am constrained until it is accomplished!' *(Lk 12:49-50)*.

The passion is evoked by two images which might seem to be opposed to each other, fire and water. In fact, these images are complementary and enable us to understand how Jesus envisaged the approaching sacrifice. Through this sacrifice he was going to enkindle the fire of love on earth in such a way that it would spread and inflame the world. He was going to plunge himself into the water of a baptism into which he would bring the whole of humanity in order to purify and renew it completely.

What he wants is not the passion in itself, but its effects: the fire definitively enkindled for the transformation of all human hearts; the baptism 'accomplished', that is, purification achieved and a new humanity created. The declaration leads us to conclude that in the life of Jesus there was an ever-growing desire to reach the end of his mission. The more involved he got in proclaiming the good news, the more he wanted to go beyond all particular situations in which he was experiencing resistance and hostility, and to accomplish at last the salvation of the world which was his ultimate objective.

This desire never ceased to grow and it must have reached its point of maximum intensity at the time of the Last Supper, immediately before the passion. We cannot make the objection that in Gethsemane Jesus begged the Father to take the chalice away from him.

That supplication shows that he was filled with terror because of the imminent torture. But his previous desire, as we have seen, was not a desire for suffering. It was a desire for what the sacrifice would bring. This desire remained, even if the anticipation of the terrible sufferings that he would undergo caused him anguish. As well as that, by telling the Father again that he accepted his will, he who was trembling in the Garden of Olives, by his conformity to the Father's plan, brought to the fore again his desire to accomplish the work of salvation, no matter what price he would have to pay.

Another nuance of Jesus' reaction to the fear which seized him because of the approaching passion appears in the Johannine account: 'Now is my soul troubled. And what shall I say? "Father, save me from this hour?" No, for this purpose I have come to this hour. Father, glorify thy name' *(Jn 12:27-28)*. The One who is about to suffer asks himself, in the anxiety which he feels, if he should beg the Father to save him from the hour foreseen for the drama of the redemption. But, immediately, he himself replies, reminding himself that it was 'for this purpose' that he had come. And since he had come expressly for that, he could not wish to be dispensed from it. His supreme desire is to glorify the Father by accomplishing the work of redemption.

So we can affirm that, in all probability, during the Last Supper Jesus was filled with the desire to enter into the baptism of the passion and to cast fire upon the earth, and that this desire was strong in his heart when events were about to take place.

Nevertheless this is not the desire that he expressed at the beginning of the meal. That was an even more intense desire, the desire to institute the Eucharist. One desire did not, in fact, cancel out the other, because the desire for the work of redemption nourished the desire for the Eucharist.

It is the desire for the Eucharist that is the more powerful one because it involves the accomplishment of the redemptive sacrifice and aims at placing the life-giving offering within people's reach. The 'earnest desire' for the Eucharist is above all the desire for a gift which contains the gift of the passion and which is destined to be multiplied indefinitely for our benefit so as to make the mystery of the death and resurrection part of our lives. This desire has all the force of the desire for the work of redemption; it also contains the powerful hope for a gift that will be perpetuated throughout human history until the end of the world.

3. The desire 'before he suffered'

The desire for a meal that would not be simply a farewell meal
By saying to his disciples that he wanted to eat the paschal meal with them before he suffered, Jesus enables us to understand better the emotion which gripped him.

We should not conclude from this that he presents the paschal meal as a simple farewell meal. Many commentators on the gospels have interpreted the Last Supper in this way. They saw it essentially as a farewell meal which took on a particularly dramatic tone. Those who wanted to reduce the mystery of Jesus as much as possible to purely human dimensions, were tempted to see the meal as that of an unforgettable man saying goodbye to his friends.

It is true that this meal was the last one that Jesus had with his disciples before he died. He himself says this: 'For I tell you I shall not eat it until it is fulfilled in the kingdom of God' *(Lk 22:16)*. However, he does not consider this last meal a simple farewell meal to end a friendship whose quality he appreciated. For him, this last Passover is destined to have its fulfilment in the kingdom. Rather than a farewell or the beginning of a separation, it is the start of a meeting on a higher level. Far from being broken, the friendship will be prolonged by being changed into relationships of a more spiritual order.

If Jesus had taken this paschal meal to be essentially a farewell meal, he would have given it a note of sadness or melancholy. But that was not his intention. He preserved the normal purpose of a meal, which was to express the joy of living together, and the normal purpose of the paschal meal, which was to celebrate the wonders of God.

During the meal he did, of course, tell his disciples about his impending death: 'But now I am going to him who sent me'. This announcement saddened his disciples — 'Because I have said these things to you, sorrow has filled your hearts' *(Jn 16:5-6)*. But the Master wanted to help his disciples to go beyond this sadness by making them understand that his going away would mean that the Holy Spirit would come to them. He adds that after having lost him at the time of his death, they will have the joy of seeing him alive again: 'A little while and you will see me no more; again a little while, and you will see me' *(Jn 16:16)*. He emphasises that their passing sadness will be transformed into ultimate joy. He does not want the climate of the paschal meal to become one of mourning.

Christ's desire then is not that of having the company of his disciples for a last time and making them experience the sadness of his leaving them. He doesn't want to anticipate, either for himself or for those he loves, the sufferings which await him at the time fixed by the Father. The food and drink which he shares with his disciples certainly do not have the bitter taste of an imminent separation.

So his desire cannot be understood as one of a goodbye full of affection for those who had followed him in his earthly pilgrimage. Jesus did not gather the twelve together at the Last Supper in the way some people gather their friends around them for the last time before they die. Of course, the closeness of death gives to the meal taken together a more striking value and charges it with emotion. But it does not plunge the Last Supper into a climate of sadness.

Jesus himself emphasises the meaning of his death when he says that there is no greater love than that of giving one's life for one's friends (Jn 15:13). He wants his love to reach its climax in sacrifice. If he had not given his life, his love could not have reached its full measure.

The last meal before his death was to celebrate this love and to show it forth. If it had taken on a note of suffering or pain it could have indicated that Jesus regretted having to offer the sacrifice of his life. Now he desired this sacrifice, because of the happiness his disciples would have as a result of it.

By means of the Eucharist he was going to ensure that the meal was not a farewell, but the beginning of innumerable meals where his disciples would find again their closeness to him. He was going to institute a source of perpetual communion in which what had been achieved by the resurrection, after the separation of death, would take on a sacramental form and in this way would be forever renewed.

So, far from being caught up in a current of sadness, this last meal was deeply orientated towards the joy of a love which wanted to give itself and which is certain of being victorious over death.

The desire for the joy of a meal
By expressing his desire to eat the paschal meal before he suffered, Jesus gave to understand that this meal would be his last joy. After the meal, suffering would come.

If he sees this meal as his last joy, it is because the whole of his life which he lived on earth with his disciples was a deep joy for him. The human existence of the incarnate Son of God was not a penance for him, as some have thought. It brought abundant joy to his human heart.

In this context we should not draw very gloomy conclusions

from the picture of the redemptive incarnation which the Letter to the Philippians gives us. Paul brings out the sacrificial aspect of the coming of the One who, while subsisting in the divine condition, emptied himself by taking on the condition of a servant or slave, and became like us (Phil 2:6-7). For one who lived in divine splendour, taking on human life is like a self-emptying or stripping. The incarnation highlights the humility of the Son of God.

However, it does not mean that the incarnate Word in his human experience only had gloomy feelings and a sad life. That is because the emptying is not a human emptying; it is that of the Son of God, who waived the manifestation of his divine glory in his human life, and who limited himself to the ordinary human condition. For the Son, the self-emptying consisted in really being a man like other men. So it did not deprive Christ of his capacity for human joy any more than it took from him a variety of human emotions and feelings.

This is how Jesus was able to experience the needs and aspirations of human nature and feel joyful when his desires were fulfilled.

The fact that he was destined for the redemptive sacrifice, where the Son of God would be even more humiliated by becoming obedient unto death, even death on the cross (Phil 2:8), could not deprive him of joy during his earthly existence. He knew that his death would be followed by his glorification and would, in this way, become a source of joy for all peoples. As well as that, he did not have to bear the weight of the passion before it came. At the Last Supper, the hour of suffering had not yet struck and Jesus was able to be joyful for the last time.

Far from being less intense than the joys of other people we can guess that Christ's joys went beyond them in density and depth. During the years at Nazareth, the child who 'increased in wisdom and in stature, and in favour with God and man' *(Lk 2:52)*, must have tasted the joy of this development. He experienced the joys of the other children of his age, but to these

44

joys were added those which were the result of his close relationship with his Father and which are revealed only in the episode which occurred when he was twelve years old. The joy of saying, 'Abba', 'Daddy', to the heavenly Father, illumined the soul of Jesus in secret. As well as that, the perfection of his life brought with it an exceptional quality of joy: his social relationships with everyone were charged with such love that they kept alive in him the joy of self-giving and developed the joyful spontaneity of devotedness.

During his public life, the framework of his life is no longer that of the family, but that of the mission, which gives to Jesus the essence of his human joy. He has the joy of carrying out the work entrusted to him by the Father; that of announcing the good news, which brings joy to his listeners, and that of multiplying the signs of divine goodness, by means of numerous miracles. He also has the joy of seeing some of those to whom he addressed his preaching, holding fast to the faith. At least on one particular occasion this joy is demonstrated in a remarkable way. It is expressed in a hymn of praise addressed to the Father. It was the hour when Jesus 'rejoiced in the Holy Spirit' *(Lk 10:21)*.

The most constant joy which Jesus experienced in his mission must have been that which came from the company of his disciples. Among his listeners there were relentless adversaries, who pursued him with hostility. There were also the crowds who, while they were captivated by his preaching, could not understand it, and allowed themselves to be won over easily by other influences. The recipients of miracles often forgot too quickly who it was who had healed them. Jesus had many disappointments. But the stable group of apostles provided a milieu where joy could be maintained and developed. We see the Master's satisfaction when, at the Last Supper, he declares to his apostles: 'You are those who have continued with me in my trials' *(Lk 22:28)*.

The Master's relationships with his disciples were based on

friendship. He did not want to treat them as servants, but as friends (Jn 15:15). While he kept his authority, he did not seek the joy of dominating, but rather that of living with those whom he loved in the greatest possible communion of soul. He opened his heart to those who accompanied him on his missionary travels and entrusted to them all that he had learned from the Father. Throughout his public life these were the joys he enjoyed with his whole human heart in a familial sharing of his whole existence.

Seeing the joys he had already experienced enables us to understand better his desire for joy at his last meal. For the last time on earth he was going to be able to express the friendship he had forged with his apostles in the most intense way. The joy which he had experienced previously in the company of his most faithful friends was going to end. The moments he was going to spend with those whom he had called to follow him and who had been fully attached to him, were going to be moments of deep happiness.

So, at the same time as he desired the paschal meal, he also desired this joy, which was going to bind him more closely to his friends.

The desire to institute the Eucharist in joy

Jesus desired to institute the Eucharist in a climate of joy. Here we find a basic clue to the very meaning of the eucharistic celebration.

The joy of the last teaching: We can imagine especially the joy that Jesus felt when, for the last time, he was giving the essential points of his doctrine. The long discourse which we find in St John constitutes the most beautiful and most substantial doctrinal development, which has come down to us from the Master. It was with joy that Christ brought light to people. Now the Eucharist gave him the opportunity to throw the most abundant light on the meaning of the work of salvation, on the roles of the Father and the Holy Spirit, on the true vine which he himself was, and on the love which should pass from his heart into the hearts of his disciples. Actually, the eucharistic mystery needs to be explained by the whole of divine action in the world, and then it clarifies the development of the Christian life in the Church. Besides, the paschal meal, with the institution of the Eucharist, gave the Master the possibility of explaining his doctrine calmly, without having to adapt it by using parables for the crowds, who were avid for images, and without having to think about the criticisms and questions of his adversaries.

Within the framework of this last meal he was able to give the form he preferred to this teaching, the form of a dialogue. In a friendly conversation with his disciples he was in a better position to answer their questions. Nowhere else in the gospel accounts do we find such a full dialogue on the part of the disciples. Several of them questioned the Master in turn. We feel that they were completely free to ask him for clarification.

So when Jesus said 'And you know the way where I am going', Thomas showed that he did not understand: 'Lord, we do not know where you are going, how can we know the way?' Then came the declaration which is so rich in meaning. 'I am the way, and the truth, and the life' *(Jn 14:4-6)*. The question was straightforward and direct, the answer was enlightening. Jesus defined what he was. Was it not a deep joy for him to be able to say so clearly what he was for all humanity? And this joy was at the same time destined to be shared by all those who would seek in him the unique way of their existence, the truth and the life. The Master showed all that the eucharistic presence brings to those who receive it.

Philip's question was more daring than Thomas's. 'Lord, show us the Father and then we will be satisfied' *(Jn 14:8)*. When he heard this request, Jesus had the satisfaction of realising that the disciple had understood well the capital importance of the Father in all his teaching. Everything depended on the Father and in him was to be found the key for explaining everything else. Above all, the Master had the joy of expressing the basic purpose of his revelation, a purpose dictated by his love for his Father. It was because he wanted to show others the Father that he came into this world, and that was what he had done his whole life. 'Have I been with you so long, and you still do not know me, Philip?' *(Jn 14:9)*. When he said this he was telling Philip that his request had been granted already and was inviting him to become aware of the favour which had been given to him — that of seeing God in a human face. For the disciple and for the others it must have been a joy to know that they had been in such intimate contact with God.

Jesus then announced a prolongation of this revelation in the lives of his disciples: 'He who has my commandments and keeps them ... I will love him and manifest myself to him' *(Jn 14:21)*. This declaration provoked a reaction in Judas: 'Lord, how is it you will manifest yourself to us, and not to the world?' We could say that the Master had used an expression which could have several meanings, 'I will manifest myself to him', in order to provoke a request for clarification. The question is important because it concerns the kind of intimate revelation of himself which Jesus will give to those who remain faithful. Once again, in a few words, the reply brought wonderful light: 'If a man loves me he will keep my word, and my Father will love him, and we will come to him and make our home with him' *(Jn 14:23)*. If Jesus is so happy to come and make his home with those who are open to him, promising this coming and this indwelling was a very special joy for him.

He made his disciples understand that it was the last time that they would be able to ask him so many questions. Soon the day would come when, having triumphed over death, he would see them again and everything would be clear. 'In that day you will ask nothing of me' *(Jn 16:23)*. On that day, which was already near, their hearts would be joyful. During the meal there was a certain anticipation of that clarity and joy. To his disciples gathered around him the Master was able to speak in plainer terms and to explain his doctrine in a clearer way. Since it was the last opportunity he would have for instructing them, he wanted to impress on their memories the essential part of his teaching and to do it in such a simple way that their minds could grasp it. The disciples themselves expressed their satisfaction with this. 'Now you are speaking plainly, not in any figure' *(Jn 6:29)*. They recognised a divine light in this clarity and they affirmed their faith in the One who was communicating the truth of God to them. 'Now we know that you know all things, and need none to question you; by this we believe that you came from God' *(Jn 16:30)*. We can imagine how joyful the Master must have been at this profession of faith, which was a response to the whole of his teaching.

So during this meal, Jesus had the joy of handing over the pure essence of his doctrine to his disciples, of seeing his teaching better understood by those who received it and of receiving their spontaneous affirmation of faith. The Last Supper ended the doctrinal work of the Saviour beautifully. After so many disappointments, and before the torment of the passion, it brought the Master the joy of seeing that his preaching had had a real result.

The joy of Christ who brought his teaching to a climax by commenting on the Eucharist was a prelude to the joy of preachers, who later on in the Church would teach the gospel message to Christians during the eucharistic celebration. And just as the disciples rejoiced at the Last Supper on receiving the illuminating words of the Master, the faithful, too, would experience the joy of receiving the light of revelation, transmitted by the messengers of the Word.

The joy of the Last Supper together: As well as the joy of the doctrinal teaching, the Last Supper brought Jesus the joy of prayer.

We remember how St Mark describes the end of the meal. 'And when they had sung a hymn, they went out to the Mount of Olives' *(Mk 14:26)*. The paschal meal ended with the singing of the Hallel. At the end of the meal, Jesus sang a hymn with his disciples. The joy of the paschal feast was expressed in this song. It was the high point of the joy that they had experienced during the meal.

This final song stands out in contrast to what was to follow. Leaving for the Mount of Olives meant leaving for darkness, where Jesus was going to tell his disciples about the sadness which suddenly overwhelmed him. 'My soul is very sorrowful even to death' *(Mk 14:34)*. A short while after the meal he was assailed by sadness.

The meal itself ended joyfully in song and prayer. We could even imagine that Jesus, knowing better than his disciples what was going to happen to him, really put his heart into singing this last prayer. He wanted to experience all the joy he could draw from it, before offering it up to the Father.

He had previously expressed his own feelings in the so-called priestly prayer with which St John ends the words spoken at the Last Supper. Actually, he could not be satisfied just to recite the prayers prescribed for the paschal meal. He did pray with his disciples, but he also wanted to mark, with a more personal prayer, the Eucharist, which he had instituted, and the great designs of hope which gave it life.

In the priestly prayer, he addressed the Father as Father, a name which was not used in the invocations of traditional Jewish prayer. The very fact of pronouncing the name 'Abba' must have given joy to Jesus, because by this name he expressed his relationship as Son to him. It was with a Son's prayer he wanted to end the meal.

In addition, in this prayer he was able to speak with ease about his mission, what he had accomplished and what still had to be done before the work of salvation was fully carried out. He opened his heart fully while looking at the Father. St John tells us that he raised his eyes to heaven, but it was to entrust to the Father the development of the kingdom on earth, and the future of the group of disciples who were with him.

Besides, he prayed before his disciples in a way that enabled them to participate as much as possible in his prayer. He wanted to make this meal a communion in friendship and through the Eucharist he conferred on this communion a new value of communion of life. So he desired communion in prayer even when he was the only one praying and was expressing his most personal intentions.

He wanted his disciples to have the same joy as he had experienced in turning towards the Father and in entrusting their whole destiny to him. He longed to be able to share with them the aspirations he was presenting to the Father. First of all he asked for the glory his resurrection was going to manifest, while declaring that he had finished the work that had been assigned to him by the Father (Jn 17:4). How could he make that declaration without joy? He rejoiced that he had fully completed his mission for the honour of the Father. He expressed the same joy when he noted the faith and fidelity of his disciples. 'They have kept thy word. Now they know that everything that thou hast given me is from thee... and know in truth that I came from thee; and they have believed that thou didst send me' *(Jn 17:6-8)*. He could not have desired a more beautiful result of his coming into the world.

He saw the work accomplished in his disciples as the communication of his own joy. After having affirmed that he had looked after his own and had kept them safe, he added: 'But now I am coming to thee; and these things I speak in the world, that they may have my joy fulfilled in themselves' *(Jn 17:13)*. In the whole of the priestly prayer he tried to ensure that this joy was shared with his disciples in the most perfect way. He prayed for their sanctification and for their unity. In asking that they be one, as he and the Father are one, he wanted the joy that came from his union with the Father to be theirs. He also wanted to bring them into the fullness of his happiness when he said: 'Father, I desire that they also, whom thou hast given me, may be with me where I am' *(17:24)*. All the joy which he received on earth from the love of the Father should go to them because of the knowledge of the Father which he had given them and would still give them: 'I made known to them thy name, and I will make it known, that the love with which thou hast loved me may be in them, and I in them' *(Jn 17:26)*.

The last words of this prayer, 'I in them', fit in very well with the purpose of the Eucharist, which is to penetrate their lives with its life and to give them its presence. They show Christ's desire to prolong into the future by means of an even more inner presence, the joy which he experienced living among his disciples.

The joy of giving himself as food and drink: When Jesus gave his body as food and his blood as drink, he gave them as fruits of a sacrificial offering. In this regard, the most explicit formula for the consecration of the bread is St Luke's 'This is my body which is given for you' *(Lk 22:19)*. It corresponds to the words used in the discourse when the Eucharist was announced: 'The bread which I shall give for the life of the world is my flesh' *(Jn 6:51)*. The flesh is given for the life of the world in the sense that it is offered as a sacrifice for humanity. The flesh of the Son of God is first of all given for the world, before being given as food to the disciples: the sacrifice preceded the meal.

It is the same for the blood — 'This is my blood of the covenant which is poured out for many' *(Mk 14:24)*. The covenant of Sinai was sealed in the blood of the animal victims (Ex 24:1-8). The unique and definitive covenant which reconciled humanity with God was sealed in the blood of Christ. This blood is first poured out for humanity, before being given as drink to the disciples.

So the words spoken by Jesus during this double consecration imply his commitment to the sacrifice of Calvary. They even presuppose an anticipation of the redemptive passion, by carrying out, as a sacrament, what would be consummated on the following day, in order to be able to communicate its fruits during a meal. When he said these words, the Saviour had before his eyes the awesome perspective of sacrifice. He was aware of the immense suffering which the institution of the eucharistic meal would cost him.

However, we have already observed that, in the soul of Jesus, this perspective of sacrifice did not mean sadness or melancholy. It was not incompatible with a more fundamental joy, that which he experienced in his self-giving. If he had not instituted the Eucharist in joy, he would have kept for himself something of what he wanted to give; he would have thought too much about the sufferings to come, that is to say, about himself, and not enough about those for whom he wished to obtain the fruits of his sufferings. In Jesus there could be none of this kind of selfishness.

It was in the pure joy of giving himself that he said, 'This is my body... this is my blood'. This joy enables us to understand better the strength of his great desire. During his public life, Jesus had awaited the moment when he could give to his disciples the most precious thing that he had — himself. When the hour came he was able to give the gift about which he had always dreamed. So he gave his disciples his body and blood with a feeling of profound happiness.

He wanted to extend his joy to his disciples. He wanted the gift of his body and blood to be received in joy and not like a present wrapped in mourning. If any gift deserved to be appreciated by the disciples it was that one. Now it was only by receiving it joyfully that they were able to show their respect and wonder for the gift that was given to them.

The Last Supper revealed in a very unobtrusive, but real way the joy of the eucharistic heart of the Saviour. This joy pertained to the perfection of his love. It illuminated, not only the institution of the Eucharist, but all subsequent eucharistic celebrations.

Jesus desired a climate of joy for these celebrations. This climate does not in any way mean that there should not be emphasis on the offering of sacrifice. The mystery which is accomplished sacramentally in the Eucharist is essentially that of the redemptive offering. So the participants are required to have an attitude of offering. But since the sacrificial offering in which the Saviour was involved did not take away from him anything of the joy of self-giving, but rather accentuated this joy by the desire to give everything, Christians who offer themselves with Jesus are invited to do so with joy. The Church understood this invitation well, when giving a festive tone to the eucharistic celebration.

It is good to point out that this joy is called for by the resurrection, inseparable from the mystery of the passion in the Eucharist. The Last Supper anticipated not just the passion, but also the resurrection and the ascension, because it was Christ, in his definitive and glorious state, who gave himself as food and drink. His body and blood could not spiritually nourish and quench the thirst of Christians if they were not, by virtue of their glorious state, filled with the Holy Spirit.

The risen Christ is a Christ who gives himself in joy and who should be received in joy. During the Last Supper, Jesus already drew from the joy of the resurrection in order to give joy to his disciples, by means of a spiritual meal. In eucharistic celebrations, this same joy should be manifested, both as a preparatory disposition, and as a fruit of the mystery.

TO EAT THIS PASSOVER WITH YOU

We can make the observation that Jesus purposely did not say, 'I have earnestly desired to institute the Eucharist'. The direct object of his great desire was 'to eat this Passover'. What he desired was to eat the paschal meal with his disciples. In order to deepen our understanding of this desire we will consider in turn, the meaning of a meal, the meaning of the paschal meal, and the meaning of the eschatological meal.

1. The meal

It is significant that Jesus desired the meal. It was under the form of a meal that he instituted the greatest of the sacraments which would contribute to the development of his Church and the life of each Christian.

We can see that for the Master this meal had a dual purpose. First of all, Jesus desired a meal because he desired to nourish the spiritual life of his disciples. In the physical order, a meal is not something optional, it is a necessity. In the spiritual domain, Jesus wanted a meal which would sustain and develop life, and the great invention of the Eucharist consisted in the gift of his own body as food. He did not want this gift to be given in a purely symbolic way, but by the real presence of his body under the appearance of bread. He desired to give people the highest possible form of spiritual food. And so that the gift of himself, which he was giving, would have its true worth, he proclaimed the need for it: 'Truly, truly, I say to you, unless you eat the flesh of the Son of man and drink his blood, you have no life in you' *(Jn 6:53)*.

He wanted to give drink as well as food. He wanted the meal to be a real one with food and drink. He also wanted to give his flesh and blood as his real human presence. Flesh and blood signify a human being. More particularly, by giving his blood under the form of wine, he desired to communicate a spiritual inebriation to his disciples. Normally, even the fact of eating causes a bodily euphoria. Wine accentuates the joy of the meal. The spiritual life needs ardour and enthusiasm in order to flower. In wanting his blood to cause inebriation of the soul, Jesus showed that the meal which he instituted was not to be one which would simply ensure survival, but one which would give abundant and even exhilarating life.

On the other hand, he desired the meal because he wanted to establish his relationships on the basis of communion. A meal fosters communion between people. We have already noted the

Master's intention of developing intimate relationships with his disciples by means of a meal.

It is this aspect of communion which receives a new basis through the words pronounced over the cup: 'This is my blood, the blood of the covenant'. By the inauguration of the covenant, the Eucharist pushed to a maximum degree the aim of communion implied in the meal. At the source of this communion it placed the covenant between God and humanity, the covenant accomplished in Jesus himself in virtue of his sacrifice. In presenting his blood as the blood of the covenant, Christ identified himself with the covenant. In him divinity and humanity were united in order to bring about union between God and human persons.

This covenant, which includes the remission of sins, reconciles us with God. At the same time, reconciliation is brought about in the relationship of the whole of humanity with the Father and in relationships between human beings. Sin had brought about a state of enmity, not only between humanity and God, but also among people themselves. It is a source of division: pride and selfishness, which set human persons against God, also cause them to oppose one another. It is therefore at the origin of all the conflicts and wars which tear apart the history of peoples and individuals.

It takes more than human effort to put an end to this destruction and to the feelings of hatred and revenge which result from it. In order to ensure peace among all peoples, peace with God must first of all be restored by obtaining pardon for our faults.

This is the reconciliation that was operated by Christ through the sacrifice of the cross and which is renewed sacramentally in the Eucharist. The Saviour becomes present as a covenant. 'For he is our peace,' writes St Paul, in affirming that, in his person, he made of the two parts of humanity, 'one new man', and destroyed hatred (Eph 2:14-16).

We can understand that Jesus intensely desired the meal where universal reconciliation was going to be manifested and where communion among people would be rooted in new-found friendship with the Father. He who knew the frailty of human beings and who had the opportunity of seeing frequent quarrels among the disciples, wanted to give a very solid foundation to unity, one which would surmount all temptations of division. His great desire was to create, through the blood of the covenant, a permanent union of which the eucharistic meal would be an effective sign.

2. The paschal meal

In the Jewish tradition, the paschal meal commemorated the liberation of the people who had been delivered from the yoke of the Egyptians. Those who awaited the Messianic event celebrated the Passover as an announcement of the liberation which the Messiah would accomplish. Jesus saw that in those around him, hope in the messianic liberation was very alive. Many were awaiting the restoration of the independence of Israel and the end of foreign occupation. In the minds of the disciples, it was this national liberation that the coming of Jesus brought closer. At the time of the ascension, they asked the Master, once again, if he were going to restore the kingdom of Israel (Acts 1:6). Their quarrels about who would have the first place should be seen in this context. The celebration of the paschal meal, by reawakening the hope of an early restoration of the kingdom, provoked a renewal of the quarrel (Lk 22:24).

Jesus had the great desire to bring about the messianic liberation, but in a completely different perspective from that of national or political restoration. He brought to humanity a much more fundamental liberation, one which would free people from the slavery of sin and give them a higher freedom, that of children of God (Jn 8:34-36). By transforming the paschal meal into the Eucharist, he wanted to enable it to obtain the benefit of this liberation for those who participated in it. He knew that, in this way, he was responding to the deepest human aspiration to liberation.

He wanted to remove the heaviest kind of slaveries from human beings — the slaveries which oppressed them in their very souls — and to allow them to taste the liberty of relating to the Father as his children.

The greatness of Christ's desire was in proportion to the entire human race's immense need for liberation. Jesus rejoiced that he was able to give the true Passover to men and women. We must realise that he did more for authentic human liberty and for deliverance from oppression and servility, than all the revolutions and all the social reforms. He alone was able to liberate what is deepest within us.

He accomplished this liberation through his sacrifice. In the paschal meal where the Eucharist was going to be instituted, he was the real lamb, which was slain for the meal. The image of the lamb had already been used by John the Baptist at the beginning of his public life: 'Behold the Lamb of God, who takes away the sin of the world!' *(Jn 1:29)*. The figure of the lamb comes from two sources, the servant of Yahweh who was compared in his sufferings to a lamb, which silently allowed itself to be led to the slaughter (Is 53:7) and the rite of the paschal meal (Ex 12). The precursor had discerned in Jesus a humble Messiah, who was as gentle as a lamb, and a Messiah, ready to allow himself to be slain like a lamb in order to purify the world from sin. Jesus knew, even better than he, what his destiny was and he wanted to take on the role of the Lamb of God. He who appeared to be like a lamb, because of his meek and humble heart, wanted to carry out to the very end the mission of a lamb in sacrifice.

The Eucharist was going to allow him to push his humility in service to its limits. When someone is God, giving himself to us as food and drink, allowing himself to be eaten and drunk by us, is a generous act which requires humility as well as the most radical availability. When he commanded the apostles to do what he was doing in memory of him, he handed over to them power over his own body and blood, and accepted the fact that he would become present on earth wherever the words of consecration were pronounced. The eucharistic presence itself bears witness to his desire to be permanently available.

Jesus' desire to make himself entirely available through the Eucharist conforms with the very meaning of the coming of the Son of man, according to the Master's declaration: 'For the Son of man also came not to be served but to serve, and to give his life as a ransom for many' *(Mk 10:14; Mt 20:28)*. The service of the Son of man was fully manifested in sacrifice. This link between sacrifice and service can be seen in the image of the lamb. By desiring a paschal meal where he would fulfil the role of the lamb, Jesus was aware that he was achieving the end for which he came into the world.

3. The eschatological meal

When he expressed his desire to eat the Passover with his disciples, Jesus used an eschatological motif: 'For I tell you, I shall not eat it until it is fulfilled in the kingdom of God' *(Lk 22:16)*. And the declaration at the close of the meal on the occasion of the fourth and last cup corresponds well to that opening one: 'I shall not drink again of the fruit of the vine until that day when I drink it new in the kingdom of God' *(Mk 14:25; Lk 22:18)*. When he said this, communion with the blood of Christ had already taken place with the distribution of the third cup, 'the cup of blessing'. Jesus had not drunk from that because he was handing over his own blood. But he drank from the final cup, saying that it was the last time he would take wine before entering the heavenly kingdom.

By framing the meal between these two eschatological statements, he showed that he considered the meal as an introduction to the heavenly banquet of the kingdom. The heavenly feast would be the fulfilment of the Passover; in heaven, what was symbolised in the paschal meal would become a reality.

In the drunkenness of heavenly joy, the new wine would succeed the last wine, which Jesus drank.

This was not the first time that Jesus evoked the heavenly banquet. He had already compared the kingdom of God to a feast organised by a king for his son's wedding (Mt 22:2). He had announced that he would come back like a master returning from a wedding and that the servants whom he found waiting would be happy: 'I say to you, he will gird himself and have them sit at table, and he will come and serve them' *(Lk 12:37)*. Likewise, the wise maidens would enter the banquet hall with the bridegroom (Mt 25:10). During the Last Supper Jesus promised his disciples: 'You may eat and drink at my table in my kingdom' *(Lk 22:30)*.

The great desire to have the paschal meal with his disciples should be seen therefore in the perspective of the heavenly banquet. The strength of this desire grows from the fact that Jesus desired the banquet in order to be able to offer it to his disciples and to get them to eat and drink at his table. He who had come to serve on earth desired to prolong this service even into the beyond by allowing his own to taste the supreme meal.

He desired to give a foretaste of the heavenly banquet in the Eucharist. By means of the eucharistic meal he receives his faithful ones at his table and gives himself to them, just as he will do in heaven, when he gives himself, with all his divine riches, for the happiness of the elect.

In fact it is the heavenly meal of the kingdom which makes the eucharistic meal possible. We have already noted that the Christ who handed himself over in the Eucharist was Christ in his glorious state. For those who find it repugnant to admit that the Son of God gave his body as food and his blood as drink, Jesus said that it is necessary to accept the mystery of the ascension, in order to be able to understand the mystery of the Eucharist. 'Do you take offence at this? Then what if you were to see the Son of man ascending where he was before?' *(Jn 6:61-62)*. It was not only the risen Lord, but the Lord ascended into heaven, and having attained the fullness of his glorification, who gave his body and blood. Jesus added: 'It is the spirit that gives life, the flesh is of no avail; the words I have spoken to you are spirit and life' *(Jn 6:63)*. The flesh of the Son of man in its earthly state of life would not have been able to nourish the life of the disciples. It would have been worthless. In order to have a nutritive value in the spiritual order, it would have to be filled with the Holy Spirit, as it is in its glorious state. The expression, 'the words I have spoken to you' could be better rendered in keeping with the semitic turn of phrase as 'the things about which I have spoken to you'. In his discourse when promising the Eucharist, Christ spoke of his body and blood as spirit and life, that is, that having been given life by the Holy Spirit, they were able to communicate spiritual life.

Thus, during the Last Supper, Jesus had the desire to organise the heavenly banquet, in order to have its savour appreciated in a veiled way in the Eucharist. What he presented in a mysterious way in the earthly eucharistic meal was the Passover fulfilled, the paschal meal having reached its perfection in heaven. In the gift of his blood as drink, he gave a taste of the new wine that he would drink in the kingdom of God.

So the joy of the Eucharist enables the disciples in a certain measure to share in the heavenly joy of Christ, the master and bridegroom of the heavenly banquet. The Eucharist should be celebrated in joy, not only because Jesus instituted it in a climate of joy, but because, in it, Christ gives his own heavenly joy of which he had a great desire to give a foretaste on earth.

3

Thanksgiving

The most fundamental indication which the gospel texts give us to help us to get to know the eucharistic heart of Jesus, concerns the thanksgiving, which immediately precedes the pronouncing of the words over the bread and wine. The great desire was only a prelude; the most intimate and most decisive state of mind and heart in the institution of the sacrament is thanksgiving. In it we find the essential meaning of the mystery. It is that which makes Christ's heart a eucharistic heart in the most literal sense of the expression, because eucharist means thanksgiving.

THE MEANING OF THANKSGIVING

1. 'He gave thanks'

If the sacrament instituted by Christ is normally called the Eucharist in Christian usage, it is because of the thanksgiving prayer which throws light on the meaning of the words of consecration and ensures their efficacy.

We should note, however, that not all the accounts of the institution give us identical words for this prayer. In the accounts of Mark (14:2) and Matthew (26:26), the verb used for the prayer said over the bread is 'to bless': 'Jesus took bread, and blessed, and broke it, and gave it to the disciples'. This verb would seem to suggest that the prayer was that in current usage in the Jewish tradition. (However, in these same accounts, the verb used for the consecration of the cup is, 'to give thanks', *eucharistesas*). Apparently the two evangelists express themselves first in the Jewish way and then change to Christian vocabulary. Would that not be a sign that at the beginning, by some instinctive attitude, the disciples tried to define the gestures and words of Jesus by referring to Jewish usages, but that finally, a new way of expressing them triumphed, a way more in keeping with the newness of Christianity?

In St Paul's account (1 Co 11:24) only the expression 'having given thanks' is used. For communion with the blood of Christ, Paul says, 'the cup of blessing which we bless' *(1 Co 10:16)*. By doing that he took up the Jewish vocabulary for the rites of the paschal meal, at which the third cup was called 'the cup of blessing'. It is even more striking that in reporting what Jesus did for the consecration, Paul did not say, 'having blessed', but 'having given thanks'. And we know that he presented his account as a tradition that went back to the Lord.

In Luke's account we find the expression, 'having given thanks', twice — the first time with regard to the cup (22:17) and the second time with regard to the bread (22:19). The first time it is said poses a problem, because the cup in question was not that of the Eucharist. It is the cup in reference to which Jesus made the eschatological statement, that is to say, the fourth cup of the meal, the last one from which he himself drank. But this would seem to be the result of confusion on the part of the evangelist; when speaking of two cups he did not distinguish sufficiently between what was said in reference to each one. For the cup of the eschatological statement, he uses what was said in reference to the eucharistic cup: thanksgiving and then the words, 'Take this, and divide it among yourselves'. We should note too that Mark and Matthew also fostered the same kind of confusion because they simply reproduce the eschatological statement after the eucharistic consecration of the cup, not knowing, apparently, that after the eucharistic cup, there was another one to end the meal. Taking into account that there was a certain confusion abut the third and fourth cups, what we must remember above all is that, according to Luke, the two consecrations of bread and wine were marked by a prayer of thanksgiving.

This confirms the fact that we cannot think of two different kinds of prayer for the two consecrations, as a superficial interpretation of Mark and Matthew would suggest. It is normal that the two consecrations should be done in an analogous way. In the tradition represented by Paul and Luke it is a question only of thanksgiving.

St John, who does not tell us about the institution of the Eucharist, but gives us an account only of the promise which was made on the occasion of the multiplication of the loaves, uses the verb 'to give thanks' to describe the prayer said by Jesus before the miracle: 'Jesus then took the loaves, and when he had given thanks, he distributed them to those who were seated' *(Jn 6:11)*. The synoptics, on the other hand, had described this same prayer as a blessing (Mk 6:41; Mt 14:19; Lk 9:16). Everything is as if the prayer of Christ had first of all been interpreted according to Jewish usage; the evangelist, who expressly presents us with the miracle as an announcement of the Eucharist, leaves aside this usage to mark the originality of Jesus' attitude of thanksgiving rather than blessing.

Consequently we notice an evolution in vocabulary. First of all there was a tendency to assimilate Jesus' prayer into a Jewish blessing. Then the emphasis was put on what distinguished the prayer from a blessing, on what made it an act proper to Jesus — an act of thanksgiving. It would seem that, as the point of departure for this evolution, we have to allow for something new which appeared in Jesus with regard to Jewish customs. There was a thanksgiving which could not be reduced simply to a blessing.

The evolution was affirmed once again after the apostolic era, because St Justin speaks of 'eucharistic nourishment', that is the bread and wine transformed into the body and blood of the Lord.[7] In this way of looking at things, the Eucharist, or thanksgiving, is considered as the prayer which causes the consecration; the transformation of the material elements shows its efficacy and highlights the difference between thanksgiving and blessing. By this we understand the motives which led the first Christians to avoid calling the prayer of Jesus a simple blessing: the newness of thanksgiving justified the newness of the mystery instituted by the Saviour, a mystery for which the Jewish religion had no parallel.

It would be good to remember this beginning of the development of the eucharistic vocabulary. To speak of 'eucharisted' bread and wine suggests that what was later called transubstantiation comes from the thanksgiving of Jesus. It is in the eucharistic heart of the Master that we must seek the secret of the 'marvellous and singular' conversion of the bread and wine into the body and blood of the Lord.[8] There is an invitation here to deepen the meaning of thanksgiving.

2. Blessing and thanksgiving

One of the great lessons which we learn from the evolution of vocabulary among the first Christians is that the gestures and words of Jesus can certainly not be interpreted by reference to the Jewish tradition alone. Some exegetes look for the key to Christ's attitudes in that tradition. Of course they are not wrong to analyse everything in Judaism which could bring light to bear on the life and teaching of Jesus. It is a necessary point of departure and much light can come from it. However, it is only a point of departure because Jesus entered the Jewish religion only to come out of it, and more precisely to come out of it at its summit. In his revelation he went beyond everything that had been taught before him, and in his action he went beyond all that the hope of the Jews had expected from the Messiah.

7. *Apologia*, 1, 66
8. The Council of Trent, Sess XIII, can 2; Denzinger-Schönmetzer, 1652.

That is why there is a considerable difference between the heart of Christ and the heart of a Jew faithful to the law. Even if we leave aside all the reproaches which could be made against many of the pious Jews who were contemporaries of Jesus, and look only at the positive aspect of their behaviour, the fact remains that he was incomparably superior to them. In his attitudes, which exteriorly could be analogous to those which were recommended by, and practised in, the Jewish religion, there was always a newness whose full value needed to be discovered and appreciated.

There was a similarity, but also an essential difference, between the prayer which Jesus said in view of the consecration of the bread and wine, and the Jewish blessing. In this regard we can note how some exegetical studies have the aim of equating thanksgiving and blessing, while others draw attention to the difference and newness. The latter show us the way to follow when they resist correlating things too quickly.

The blessing *(berakah)* played an important role in Jewish worship. It had a double direction, downward and upward. In the downward direction, God blessed the people by manifesting his favour to them and ensuring them of many advantages of all kinds. In the upward direction, the Jews blessed God by recognising his favours and by proclaiming his divine omnipotence. Blessing God, who blesses us, was then the double direction of the blessing based on the reciprocity of relationships between God and humanity.

This blessing takes on a new value in the context of the coming of Christ and of his work. We find a remarkable illustration of this in the hymn which opens the epistle to the Ephesians. St Paul blesses God the Father because of the blessings he has poured out on humanity through his beloved Son: 'Blessed be the God and Father of our Lord Jesus Christ, who has blessed us in Christ with every spiritual blessing in the heavenly places' *(Eph 1:3)*. He indicates what these blessings consist of. Before the foundation of the world he destined us in love to be his adopted sons in Christ. Through Christ, whose sacrifice obtained for us the remission of our sins, he filled us with his grace and through him he wants to restore and unify the whole universe, to 'recapitulate' it. By the richness of its expression, the hymn tries to highlight the marvellous abundance of divine blessings by insisting on the absolute sovereignty of the Father, who established his plan before all time and carried it out in accordance with his will. The whole work of salvation, like the hymn itself, is destined for 'the praise of glory' of the Father (Eph 1:12-14).

So we see how the Jewish blessing has not lost its *raison d'être* in Christian worship but is fully echoed in the light of the work carried out by the Saviour according to the Father's plan. As it stands the prayer which Jesus said over the bread and wine could be simply a blessing. But it was called thanksgiving; there was something more in it than a blessing.

Thanksgiving consists in being grateful. It is significant that in Jewish religious vocabulary there was no special word for expressing an attitude of gratitude to God, for saying 'thank you'.[9] Sometimes the translations of biblical texts mention thanksgiving, but this translation does not correspond exactly to the terms used. More especially the sacrifices of *todah* have been interpreted as thanksgiving sacrifices, but nevertheless we have to say that this was not their precise meaning. *Todah* could be translated by several terms, none of which really means thanksgiving.[10]

The lack of a correct term meaning thanksgiving is significant. It does not imply that the attitude of thanksgiving was absent from Jewish religious dispositions of soul. We can remember especially the cry of the psalmist, 'What shall I render to the Lord for all his bounty to me?' *(Ps 116:12)*. But it was rather a blessing or praise which summarised what was essential in the

---

9. cf C. Giraudo, *La Struttura letteraria della preghiera eucaristica*, Rome, 1981.
10. cf H. Cazelles, *Eucharistie, benediction et sacrifice dans l'Ancien Testament,* in *Maison-Dieu,* 123 (1975), 19

Jewish attitude before divine favours. The Jew blessed God, or 'confessed' him by exalting his omnipotence and proclaiming the wonders of his goodness.

We must analyse more closely what was new about thanksgiving and what distinguished it from blessing. We know from experience what 'thank you' means, but we have to make an effort to understand all it means in relationships with God in order to discern better the real meaning of the 'eucharistic' attitude of Jesus.

3. Praise and thanksgiving

For the Jews, blessing in the upward direction was praise addressed to God. This praise has unquestionably produced beautiful expression of the Jewish religious soul.

At a first glance we could even think that praise goes beyond all other forms of religious sentiment, especially thanksgiving. Actually, when we thank God we think of what we have received from him, whereas when we praise him do we not detach ourselves more from ourselves to contemplate divine wonders? Praise could seem to be a more disinterested prayer than thanksgiving, a prayer in which we forget ourselves and think only of what God has done.

In actual fact, in their praise, the Jews were far from forgetting the favours they had received from God. They always remembered the great things the Lord had done for his people, their liberation from the yoke of Egypt especially, but also all the happy events of their history. Certain individual prayers of praise, like the one contained in Psalm 22, have as a motif the divine loving-kindness which answered a supplication. 'I will tell of thy name to my brethren; in the midst of the congregation I will praise thee.... For he (Yahweh) has not despised or abhorred the affliction of the afflicted; and he has not hid his face from him, but has heard when he cried to him' *(Ps 22:22,24).*

So praise is not completely disinterested. It appreciates God more particularly in the gifts which he give us. But it has the characteristic of exalting the divine greatness, the absolute sovereignty with which God conceives and carries out his plans. It loves to proclaim the incomparable superiority of divine wisdom and how incomprehensible it is to human intelligence. But while it admires the divine goodness, it does so by contemplating the way its loving-kindness gives so freely. In a general way, it tends to emphasise the distance which separates God from humanity.

We see that praise occupied an essential place in Jewish piety, since the revelation addressed to the chosen people tended to promote faith in a God who was unique and sovereign. It showed the gap between creatures and their creator. In order to give a greater assurance of faith, divine transcendence had to appear in its full light and people had to feel completely surpassed by a God whom they had to honour by fearing him. Praise shows a kind of attachment to God which does not try to lessen the distance, but to emphasise it more by the celebration of divine wonders.

Thanksgiving on the other hand supposes that God and people draw closer together. This happens because the emphasis is placed on communion, on relationships of intimacy, or because the awareness of favours received gives rise spontaneously to gratitude.

It therefore implies a situation where God wishes to overcome the distance which separated him from humanity. In fact this distance was accentuated in the Old Testament only so that it would be closed up by the coming of Christ. God revealed his transcendence only so that he could show better to what extent his omnipotence desired to place itself at our disposal. In the heart of Christ, the Son of man, who had come to serve, showed that the One who held perfect sovereignty, wanted to be absolutely available. At the same time, Jesus unveiled the love of the Father, who watches closely over us and our needs. In him the distance disappears, because God and a human being are united in the same person.

When it is aware of the divine gift which comes to it in Christ, humanity feels invited to give thanks. It cannot be content just with praising God by exalting his greatness. It has to thank him by expressing its appreciation for a love which willed to be so close to it. To give thanks means to enter more profoundly into the warmth of an offered love. It means taking part in an exchange which God wished to establish when he came close to us. We recognise the goodness whose effects we experience, and in saying 'thank you' we respond by a homage of love. Through thanksgiving we give something back to God for his favours. In gratitude there is an awareness of being able to please God by thanking him, of being able to give him joy, and of being able to give oneself to him in return for the gift received. We are so sure of the closeness and the loving-kindness of God that we offer ourselves to him in return.

Thanksgiving accentuates reciprocity in mutual love. We have already noted a reciprocity in the blessing, through the bond which exists between the blessing which descends on people from God, and that which ascends from people in praise to God. In the same way, thanksgiving implies a grace which comes from God. But what is specific to this gratitude is that it is aware of giving something to God. God loved the world so much that he gave it the ability to give him joy by its gratitude. It means that thanksgiving pushes love in communion to its limits.

4. The perfection of thanksgiving in Jesus

If thanksgiving is a characteristic attitude of the most complete communion between God and humanity, we must say that it was present in Jesus. It is in him that the most integral thanksgiving is shown forth. He had to be the first to enter into this disposition in order to draw all humanity after him.

However, in Jesus thanksgiving takes on an exceptional physiognomy since he is a divine person, the Son. It is not simply a human attitude of gratitude towards God; it goes from the Son to the Father. It is a truly human thanksgiving, but it has an infinite value since it comes from One who is God.

If we consider Jesus' position before the Father, we note how much he emphasised that he owed everything to the Father about whom he spoke constantly. He regarded himself as the Father's envoy and he spent his whole earthly life on a mission which had its origin in the Father. He did not only give his own authority as the guarantee of his teaching since this was the authority of a Son who received everything from the Father: 'What I say, therefore, I say as the Father has bidden me' *(Jn 12:50)*. During the Last Supper he told his disciples that he had made known all that he had heard from the Father (Jn 15:15). His action is like that of the Father because 'the Father loves the Son, and shows him all that he himself is doing' *(Jn 5:20)*. The wonderful works which he accomplished, especially the miracles, were a gift from his Father. He called them 'the works which the Father has granted me to accomplish' *(Jn 5:36)*. Moreover, Jesus also said that the Father was present in him (Jn 10:38) by means of a continual presence which accompanied him constantly in his activity. Jesus was never left alone in solitude (Jn 8:29). He possessed all that belonged to the Father: 'All mine are thine', he said to him; and on another occasion he declared, 'All things have been delivered to me by my Father' *(Mt 11:27; Lk 10:22)*.

Thus the awareness that he had received everything from the Father is one of the things that strikes us most in Jesus' behaviour. We could even say that it is his most fundamental characteristic. In no other human awareness could we find such a living conviction of a divine gift which gives life to all existence and all activity. It was essentially his awareness of being the Son which discerned in everything a gift which came from the Father's love.

Even what was most personal in him had its origin and explanation in the Father. That is why, at the Last Supper, he decreed a 'new commandment' *(Jn 13:34)*, which he called 'my commandment' *(Jn 15:12)*: 'Love one another as I have loved you'. He added that this would be the sign by which his disciples would be known (Jn 13:35). It would be in some way his personal mark on their conduct. Now this love came from the Father: 'As the Father has loved me, so I have loved you' *(Jn 15:9)*. From then on, the personal mark which he would imprint on the life of mutual love of his disciples would be the mark of the Father. Since all love comes from the Father, he purposely gave the Father as the model to be followed: 'Love your enemies and pray for those who persecute you, so that you may be sons of your Father who is in heaven; for he makes his sun rise on the evil and on the good, and sends rain on the just and on the unjust' *(Mt 5:44)*. It is his own commandment, 'But I say to you', and it is entirely within the perspective of the prolongation of the Father's love.

Jesus saw the whole paschal drama as having its origin in this love. At the moment of his arrest he told Peter to leave aside all armed resistance: 'Shall I not drink the cup which my Father has given me?' *(Jn 18:11)*. This cup was one of pain, but since, in the perspective of Jesus, the passion and death result in the resurrection, the cup evoked 'the cup of salvation', which the psalmist raised in honour of Yahweh, in the offering of the sacrifice of praise (Ps 116:13). Jesus awaited the resurrection as the glorification given by the Father through his death (Jn 17:1).

This way of constantly recognising the Father's gift is part of the attitude of thanksgiving. The word 'recognition' implies first of all the discernment of the favours received. Jesus was always in a state of discernment.

The other aspect of thanksgiving is formed by the homage which is given in return for what has been received. Now among all those who give thanks for divine favours, Jesus was the only one who was able to give back in homage as much as he had received. He had received everything from the Father and he gave everything back to him. By means of his thanksgiving, he gave back completely all that which had been given to him, so that there was an equality between the grace received and the thanksgiving.

We must emphasise that here we are far removed from a thanksgiving which limited itself to a word of thanks. Thanksgiving involved the whole person of Jesus in the gift which he made of himself to the Father. Jesus kept nothing for himself from what the Father had given him. He gave the Father everything he had and was.

So he did not limit himself to declaring that he was loved by the Father: In carrying out his Father's will, he responded to the Father's love with his own (Jn 15:10). That is why 'I do as the Father has commanded me so that the world may know that I love the Father' *(Jn 14:31)*. He lived because of the Father (Jn 6:57), not only in the sense that he received his life from the Father, but also because his whole heart, mind and will were turned towards the Father and in that sense the Father was the reason for his earthly existence.

The reciprocity in equality between what came from the Father and what was offered to him is well marked in several declarations. It is the case of presence or mutual immanence: 'The Father is in me and I am in the Father' *(Jn 10:38; 14:10)*. The Father gave himself to Jesus by living in him, and Jesus in his turn offers his whole presence to the Father. It is the same thing for mutual belonging: 'All mine are thine, and all thine are mine' *(Jn 17:10)*. In order to understand better the meaning of thanksgiving, we must invert the two statements because the Father first of all gives his own riches to Christ, then Christ offers them to him in return. Their reciprocal recognition (thanksgiving) is no less characteristic: 'No one knows the Son except the Father and no one knows the Father except the Son and anyone to whom the Son chooses to reveal him' *(Mt 11:27)*. It is the Father who makes the Son known to the little ones and it is Jesus who recognises the Father in their belonging and makes him known through his revelation to humanity. These examples of reciprocity in equality show how the Father gave everything to his incarnate Son and how he offered everything back to him in return.

Consequently, we discern in Christ the ideal of thanksgiving, the absolute summit which thanksgiving can attain. Because he is the Son, he was able, in his homage of gratitude, to equal the love which the Father had bestowed on him, and to offer him unreservedly all that he had received from his goodness. Only the mystery of the Incarnation could make such a perfect thanksgiving possible.

FROM THANKSGIVING TO THE EUCHARIST

St John presents us with certain landmarks in the thanksgiving journey of Jesus.

1. Thanksgiving in the multiplication of loaves and the promise of the Eucharist

We have already seen how John is the only evangelist who presents the prayer before the multiplication of the loaves as a prayer of thanksgiving. He is also the only one who reports the commentary which Jesus made on this miracle as the announcement of the Eucharist. Now, in that commentary the Master emphasised strongly that our true food, the food that will give us eternal life, comes from the Father.

Of course, Jesus first said that this food came from himself. It actually consisted of the body and blood of the Son of God. He recommended to the crowds who followed him in the hope of an indefinite multiplication of material bread, that they try rather to obtain 'the food which endures to eternal life, which the Son of man will give to you' *(Jn 6:27)*. But he added immediately that the Son of man was marked with the Father's seal, that is to say, consecrated by the Father in the flesh and blood which was going to nourish humanity. That means that this food was prepared by the Father. Afterwards Jesus said this even more clearly: 'Truly, truly I say to you, it was not Moses who gave you the bread from heaven; my Father gives you the true bread from heaven' *(Jn 6:32)*.

More than that even, he recognised the Father's gift in yet another way when he said: 'All that the Father gives me will come to me' *(Jn 6:37)*. Here he was speaking of those who believed in the Eucharist and who would come to him to obtain it. So, in Jesus' way of looking at things, it was not only the eucharistic bread which came from the Father — the eucharistic assembly was also a gift which the Father entrusted to him. The same would hold good for every community which would come together in the future to celebrate the mystery. It is the Father who draws them to the meal: 'No one can come to me unless the Father who sent me draws them' *(Jn 6:44)*.

When many of the disciples murmured, on hearing of the need to eat the flesh of the Son of God and drink his blood, Jesus said regretfully: 'But there are some of you that do not believe'. And then he added: 'This is why I told you that no one can come to me unless it is granted him by the Father' *(Jn 6:64-65)*. So he received as a fruit of the Father's gift, those who believed in the Eucharist.

Finally, he refers back to the Father, the primary source of life, to attribute to him the origin of the eternal life, which would be communicated to the one who would eat his body and drink his blood: 'As the living Father sent me, and I live because of the Father, so he who eats me will live because of me' *(Jn 6:57)*. It is the eucharistic Jesus who will enable the disciple who eats of him to live, but the life he communicates comes from the Father.

In that way, by announcing the institution of the sacrament, his attitude was essentially one of thanksgiving. He recognised the Father's gift in everything which would constitute the Eucharist: the bread from heaven which is the flesh of the Son of God, the faith of those who would come to him, and the life-giving effect of the eucharistic meal.

In fact, the eucharistic discourse clarifies retrospectively the meaning of the thanksgiving prayer before the distribution of the loaves to the crowd. It confirms the fact that it was not a simple ritual prayer before a meal, but was the expression of Jesus' deepest state of mind and heart, as he was aware of inaugurating, by means of a symbol, the gift of the Eucharist which he saw as coming from the generosity of the Father.

2. Thanksgiving for the raising of Lazarus

After he had asked that the stone in front of the tomb be taken away, and even before he worked the miracle, Jesus raised his eyes to heaven and said: 'Father, I thank thee that thou hast heard me' *(Jn 11:41)*.

We could be surprised by this invocation publicly addressed to the Father. In fact, he had demanded an act of faith centred on his own person from Martha, to whom he had announced the raising of her brother. For the immediate raising from the dead of Lazarus, they had to believe in the One who was there and who possessed the source of life within himself: 'I am the resurrection and the life: he who believes in me, though he die yet shall he live, and whoever lives and believes in me shall never die. Do you believe this?' *(Jn 11:25-26)*. We must remember that Martha was tending towards this faith, because she had already said to Jesus: 'I know that whatever you ask from God, God will give you' *(Jn 11:22)*.

Jesus wanted to make use of this opening in his reply, but he asked Martha to go another step forward in faith. It was not just a question of believing that God was ready to give everything to Jesus, but of believing in Jesus himself who was the resurrection and, as such, was God. Martha understood this request because she said: 'Yes Lord; I believe that you are Christ the Son of God, who is coming into this world' *(Jn 11:27)*. Just before the miracle, Jesus reminded her once again about the necessity of faith. 'Did I not tell you that if you would believe you would see the glory of God?' *(Jn 11:40)*. Faith in Jesus should facilitate the manifestation of the divine glory which he has at his disposal.

Now in spite of this insistence on faith in his own person, Jesus showed that it was from the Father that he obtained the miracle of the raising of Lazarus. Since he had presented himself as the resurrection, those who were there could have thought that he did not need anyone else to work the miracle. If he possessed the source of life within himself, why did he have recourse to the Father?

Here we grasp the objective of Jesus' revelation. He wanted to show that he was God and that was why he demanded faith in himself. Strictly speaking he was not a man who should ask God for the miracle of the raising of Lazarus. He was the Son of God who possessed the divine power to raise from the dead. But since he was the Son of God, he received everything from the Father. So it was as the incarnate Son of God that he asked the Father for the miracle which he was going to order of his own authority by crying: 'Lazarus, come out' *(Jn 11:43)*.

This is also the reason why he was not afraid of a refusal, as the words following the thanksgiving show: 'I knew that thou hearest me always, but I have this on account of the people standing by, that they may believe that thou didst send me' *(Jn 11:42)*. The thanksgiving, said before the miracle, shows that Jesus was certain that it was going to take place.

The importance of this miracle lies in the fact that it is a prelude to, and an announcement of, Jesus' own resurrection. The One who worked this miracle, having declared that he was the Resurrection, showed his power to find life through death. Shortly beforehand he had said about his life: 'I have power to lay it down, and I have power to take it again'. He added nevertheless: 'This charge I have received from my Father' *(Jn 10:18)*. Thus he considered his personal power of resurrection as a power received from the primary authority, his Father.

From this we see that the thanksgiving for the raising of Lazarus from the dead is for something more than that, it is also for Jesus' resurrection. It is a thanksgiving addressed beforehand to the Father for the crowning event of the work of salvation. Jesus would not be on earth just before rising from the dead and therefore would not be able to make a prayer of thanksgiving. This prayer had already been made at the tomb of Lazarus when the stone was removed and did not need to be repeated.

We can still wonder why this thanksgiving was made before the miracle rather than afterwards. We could think that it would be more logical for Jesus to address his thanksgiving to the Father, when he had seen his friend Lazarus alive again.

A first reason of a practical order could be advanced. It was at the most intense moment, in the silent waiting, when all eyes were fixed on him, that Jesus wanted to pay homage to the Father, through the miracle he was going to work. At that moment he was able to get people to understand more easily his relationship as Son to the Father, and to show that the Father was the primary author of the miracle. Once Lazarus had come out of the tomb, the explosion of joy from the bystanders would have prevented him from drawing attention to his relationship with the Father. All attention would be on the person raised from the dead, either in stupefaction or in admiration.

However, there could have been another reason why the thanksgiving was made before the miracle. At the time of the multiplication of the loaves, Jesus had given thanks before working the miracle. And at the time of the institution of the Eucharist, he would give thanks before changing bread and wine into his body and blood. By making the deep offering of himself in thanksgiving, Jesus opened himself more completely to the Father, so that he could use his divine power and work the miracle.

We need to point out the affinity between the thanksgiving which preceded the raising of Lazarus and that which marked the Last Supper. The first Eucharist implied, in effect, an anticipation of the resurrection of Jesus, an anticipation which was necessary if the flesh and blood of the Saviour were to be given in a glorious and living state. In both cases, then, the thanksgiving points to the mystery of the resurrection.

3.   Thanksgiving in returning to the Father

When he gives an account of the Last Supper, St John draws the attention of his readers to the awareness which Jesus had that he was returning to the Father. He knew that 'his hour had come to depart out of this world to the Father' *(Jn 13:1)*. It was also the hour in which he loved his own 'to the end'. His return to the Father was going to be carried out through a way of love reaching the maximum point of sacrifice.

The evangelist is concerned above all to show that Jesus was not simply the victim of Judas' betrayal and that his death was not principally due to unfortunate circumstances. He knew 'that the Father had given all things into his hands, and that he had come from God and was going to God' *(Jn 13:3)*.

In these few words we see Jesus' fundamental attitude of mind and heart which formed his thanksgiving. He was aware that he had received everything from the Father and that he was returning to him as he had come from him. Since he does not recount the institution of the Eucharist, very probably because he did not want to repeat what had been said in the other gospels, the evangelist does not have the opportunity to say expressly that Jesus gave thanks. But he shows us that the thanksgiving was not just a moment of prayer and that it expressed the depths of the Saviour's soul, his deepest attitude of heart and mind.

It is true that the awareness of going from this world to the Father could mean that Jesus simply saw that death was approaching and that he was going into the beyond. But he showed clearly that he was not going to the sacrifice against his will. He found it normal to go to the Father, precisely because he had come from the Father. Death had a different meaning for him than for others, because before coming into the world he was with the Father and his home was the Father's home: 'I came from the Father and have come into the world; again, I am leaving the world and going to the Father' *(Jn 16:28)*. Returning to the Father was the ultimate consequence of having left his side. There was a proportion between the two events.

We have noted that in Jesus thanksgiving implied an equality between what was received from the Father and what was offered to him. Here we see this equality between leaving (the Father) and returning to him. When returning to the Father Jesus wanted to offer to him all that he had been when he came into this world. Thanksgiving included not only all that he possessed, but all that he was.

As well as that, Jesus went to the Father willingly. In fact, he said to his disciples: 'If you loved me, you would have rejoiced, because I go to the Father; for the Father is greater than I' *(Jn 14:28)*. On his return he had the joy of meeting his Father again, and the joy of offering himself in a love filled with thanksgiving.

The statement 'the Father is greater than I' must be understood within the framework of the revelation which Jesus gave of his divinity as a Son, who owed everything to the Father. Since he was God and received everything from the Father, he could not be less perfect than the Father. But because he received this perfection from the Father, the Father is greater than he: the Son had come from him and was now going back to him. It is therefore because of priority of origin that the Father is greater. He is the point of departure and in this way is also the point of arrival.

Jesus rejoiced that he was going to the Father because all his love as Son drew him towards him. Since he had received his whole human life from him, he wanted to bring it back to him as an offering, by rejoining him in his eternal home. His joy was part of the intensity of his thanksgiving.

His priestly prayer was brought to life by the intention of glorifying the Father through his sacrifice. In it he told of what had been given to him by the Father and, even where he did not mention the Father by name, when he spoke about the imminence of his sacrifice, his intention was always to offer himself to him. When he said, 'For their sake I consecrate myself' *(Jn 17:19)*, he took this consecration to mean the consummation of his belonging to the Father in his human life. Whoever is 'sacred' or 'holy' is the one who belongs to God. For Jesus, to consecrate himself or to sanctify himself meant carrying out fully his belonging to the Father through sacrifice. Here again we see the fundamental disposition of giving back to the Father as an offering, all that he had given him.

THANKSGIVING IN THE EUCHARIST

1. Thanksgiving and the eucharistic consecration

Now that we have highlighted the depth of thanksgiving in Jesus, we must examine its influence on the eucharistic consecration. This influence is expressed most especially, as we have seen, in the terminology used by St Justin: the 'eucharisted' nourishment, that is to say, the bread and wine transformed through thanksgiving into the body and blood of Christ.

It goes without saying that if thanksgiving meant simply a homage of gratitude to the Father, it could not produce such an important effect. But it included an offering which sought to give back to the Father what had come from him, and in the case of Christ this offering implied the complete giving of the person, a gift which succeeded in restoring integrally to the Father all that had been received from him. Thanksgiving mobilised all the forces of his personality in the most perfect offering.

It was accomplished in the consecration which Christ made of himself. We should note that in order to accomplish the consecration of the bread and wine, Jesus had especially consecrated himself according to the statement which we have already mentioned — 'For their sake I consecrate myself'. His thanksgiving committed him fully to the redemptive sacrifice, a sacrifice which demanded all his vital energy, as is shown by the acceptance of the Father's will in Gethsemane, which was paid for so dearly by an inner struggle.

It is true that the climate of the Last Supper was very different from that of the Garden of Olives. We have had the opportunity of pointing this out, by contrasting the joyful atmosphere of the last meal with the anguish which so soon afterwards enveloped the Master's soul. But the thanksgiving included commitment to the passion and the words said over the bread and wine showed this very clearly.

When Jesus said 'This is my body which is given for you' *(Lk 22:19)*, he showed the objective of thanksgiving; he wanted to offer himself to the Father for the benefit of humanity in a sacrifice which would ensure the presence of his body. In the same way the words, 'This is my blood of the covenant, which is poured out for many' *(Mk 14:24)*, indicated clearly the offering of a blood sacrifice in the presence of his blood. These words could obtain their efficacy only from the personal offering which Jesus made of himself.

So we can understand why thanksgiving exercises a decisive influence over the changing of bread and wine into the body and blood of Christ. It is because it involves a total offering of Jesus which causes his presence in his flesh and blood. The words of consecration certainly had their effect, but they had it only in virtue of the sacrifice. The One who consecrated himself for humanity could consecrate bread and wine in view of nourishing us with his own life.

It is useful to remember that in the eucharistic celebration the presence of the body and blood could not be dissociated from the offering of the sacrifice. The body and blood did not become present simply in virtue of the principle that the words of consecration produce their effect as soon as they are said; the presence is acquired by reason of the offering and in the offering itself. There is a sacramental renewing of the sacrifice which is accomplished because of the words which have a determining efficacy on the presence, in so far as they signify the making present of the offering of Calvary.

Neither should we lose sight of the double perspective of thanksgiving in regard to this efficacy. We have emphasised above all the offering which it includes, but it presupposes, primarily, the recognition of the Father's gift. Now the Father's gift attains a supreme degree of generosity in the fact that the body and blood of Christ become present. The Father, who had given his Son to the world through the mystery of the incarnation, gives him again in the multiple eucharistic celebrations. During the Last Supper, Jesus was aware that he was disposing of this gift of the Father, and of giving it to the end. When he proclaimed the presence of his body and blood, it was in virtue of a thanksgiving in which he had recognised the Father's will to obtain this spiritual food for humanity.

Changing bread and wine into a body and blood is an operation which requires creative power, an absolute domination which is able to change the substance of things. Jesus exercised this power but with an essential attitude of thanksgiving; he recognised that he owed the Father the body and blood which were going to be distributed as food and drink.

By this we understand better why the sacrament instituted by Jesus deserves to be called the Eucharist. The thanksgiving did not have a secondary role as an introductory prayer to the essential rite of consecration. The fundamental attitude of thanksgiving which Jesus adopted during the Last Supper contributed to the effect of the rite. In some way it gave to the food and drink an essentially 'eucharistic' quality of gratitude for the Father's gift and for the total offering in sacrifice. The sacrament flowed from what was deepest in Jesus' soul, his relationship as Son to the Father. It was because Christ's heart was perfectly eucharistic that he gave birth to the Eucharist for the Church.

2. The reflection of Christ's eucharistic disposition in Christians

Thanksgiving, which played an important role in the institution of the Eucharist to the point of giving it its name, was destined to pass from Christ to all who would take part in eucharistic celebrations. If there is to be deep participation, the participants should try to have the Saviour's sentiments and enter into the mystery of his eucharistic heart, to make his disposition their own.

With Christ, Christians should make the effort to recognise the Father's gift. Everything they have comes from the Father. It is not enough to recognise him as their Creator who gives them existence and life at every moment, and places the world around them at their disposal. Above all, they should discern in him their Father, the Father of Jesus, who is the Father of each one of them as well, according to the formula used by the risen Lord: 'My Father and your Father' *(Jn 20:17)*. From this Father they have received everything which forms their spiritual life in them. It is he who sent his Son into the world to save and sanctify it; it is he who pours the Holy Spirit into their hearts by communicating divine love to them. It is because of this free generosity of the Father that they can affirm that all is grace. Everything, both in the universe and in themselves is given to them by a sovereign goodness.

As well as that they are invited by Jesus to recognise the signs of the attentive presence of the Father in events. The Father, in fact, provides for all their needs so they can banish all anxiety (Mt 6:25-34). The Father, who gives each flower a garment more beautiful than Solomon's royal purple and who feeds the birds, watches over the lives of his children with much more care. He is interested in the smallest details of their daily existence and nothing escapes his watchfulness. Not a hair can fall without his permission (Mt 10:29-30). So all Christians can discover with the eyes of faith, not only the signs of God, but, more precisely, the signs of the Father and of his fatherly love in everything which happens to them.

Through this effort of perceiving in a real way the presence of the Father in all things, a habitual disposition of thanksgiving is formed. The Christian enters into the optic of the Master who lives his human life as an ongoing gift from the Father.

Even in painful events the Christian should still recognise the Father's mysterious gift, just like Jesus, who always saw his sacrifice as a work willed by the Father. The Eucharist manifests this truth particularly because in it thanksgiving means a commitment to the redemptive sacrifice. This commitment takes nothing away from the disposition of gratitude for the Father's gift; it confirms it to the end.

For the Christian, as for Jesus, thanksgiving is not limited to saying 'thank you' to the Father. It implies the will to give him back as much as possible of what he has given and, consequently, a personal offering. An offering made in a spirit of thanksgiving cannot be accomplished unwillingly or simply out of necessity. It has to be motivated by joy and aroused by the enthusiasm of the heart of a child, who sees itself overwhelmed by the Father's favours.

The Eucharist helps to develop this disposition of offering in union with that of the Saviour, in the joy of a sacrifice which will culminate in the resurrection and ascension, the supreme climax given by the Father to the drama of the passion. Thanksgiving touches the depths of the human soul only when it gives the Father the homage of the whole person, without wishing to avoid the suffering which this homage implies. It attains its fullness only when it rejoices to be able to give everything to the Father.

It is expressed more easily wherever family relationships are established with the Father. Jesus, who in all his prayers called the Father 'Daddy', was committed to thanksgiving with the intense love of a Son. He loved his Father so much that in his gratitude he wanted to give him everything. The more that Christians have family relationships with the Father, the more their spontaneity as children impels them to thanksgiving like Jesus. Such Christians are more constantly aware of the goodness of God and they feel led to respond by the generosity of their offering.

Finally, Christians are called in thanksgiving to be aware of the need that others have of their offering. In giving thanks, Christ offered himself for the salvation of humanity. Because of this, the Father was pleased with his homage, since the Father is the first to desire the salvation of humanity. Christians who want to bear witness to their gratitude to the Father place themselves at his disposal, as Christ did in an offering which is destined to obtain liberation and a more abundant life for others.

4

The development of the paschal mystery in the life of Jesus

We have noted the link which existed between Jesus' great desire and the feast of the Passover: 'I have earnestly desired to eat this Passover with you...' *(Lk 22:15)*.

This desire was expressed as the desire of that moment. Jesus was not speaking directly of a previous desire that had continued. In the Greek text of the gospel, the verb used for 'I have desired' signifies a momentary or transitory disposition.[11] It was the desire which arose in the Saviour's heart at that moment.

However, since it was a powerful desire which appeared with exceptional force, we must realise that it was not something which happened suddenly. It was the fruit of a whole inner development. In a way, it is a desire which broke out after it had been formed quietly and it was expressed in a vivid and moving way after a whole silent preparation.

Now since this desire was to eat the Passover, we must try to reconstruct some characteristics of the celebration of Passover feasts which must have nourished and developed the desire to institute the Eucharist. If the great desire was linked to the last Passover feast, we can reasonably suppose that the previous Passover feasts had helped to fire and strengthen it.

Here we find a precious clue which enables us to penetrate

11. The verbal form is the aorist one: *epethumesa*.

the development of the eucharistic heart. Of course Passover feasts were external celebrations, but some of them were marked by words and actions of Jesus and provide us with the opportunity to meditate on the Saviour's deep state of mind and heart in the perspective of the Eucharist.

THE FIRST PASSOVER OF JESUS MENTIONED IN THE GOSPEL

1. The annual pilgrimage to Jerusalem

The only episode which has been recorded for us in the gospel texts about Jesus' youth is the incident which happened on the occasion of a pilgrimage to Jerusalem for the feast of the Passover.

'Now his parents', Luke tells us, 'went to Jerusalem every year at the feast of the Passover. And when he was twelve years old they went up according to custom' *(Lk 2:41-42)*. We could wonder if Jesus went to Jerusalem for the first time when he was twelve years old, or if he had already accompanied his parents there. The evangelist does not say that it was his first pilgrimage, and very probably he would have said so if that were the case. Also the details given later would lead us to think that it was not his first time. Joseph and Mary were not worried about Jesus when they saw that he wasn't with them. They thought that he was in the company and made a whole day's journey without checking. This attitude would seem to indicate that they had previously come with Jesus and that the twelve-year-old child knew the customs. They had no need to watch over him specially.

From this we can conjecture with probable accuracy that ever since Jesus was able to go with them, Mary and Joseph had gone with him each year to Jerusalem for the Passover feast. They took him with them as soon as possible at a young age, because they did not want to be separated from him or leave him at Nazareth. We can imagine with what secret fervour Jesus would have participated in the pilgrimage, celebrated the feast in Jerusalem and eaten the paschal meal with his parents. This pilgrimage was a break in the everyday life of Nazareth. For Mary and Joseph it was the great event of the year. They desired this journey and prepared for it carefully. We can imagine that it made an even greater impression on the child. Jesus remembered each pilgrimage and earnestly desired the one of the following year. We could speak of his having a great desire even at that time: 'I have earnestly desired to eat this Passover...'

However, here we must ask an essential question. Did Jesus participate in the celebration of the Passover feast in the same way as the other Jews who went to Jerusalem? Or had the pilgrimage another meaning for him?

The words he said when he was twelve years of age show that the Temple had an extraordinary value for him, not simply because it was God's house, but because it was his Father's house. Now he must have understood what he said at this age since the time he began going to Jerusalem on pilgrimage. When he arrived in the Temple he experienced a joy that no one else knew, a joy which surpassed that of Mary and Joseph and which was totally personal. There he met the One he called 'Abba' in his intimate dialogue and prayer, the One who was his 'Daddy'.

Could Jesus have gone into the Temple without recognising it as his Father's house? Here we can apply a principle which governs all child psychology. Jesus always lived in the truth. As soon as his awareness was developed as a child, he became aware that he was the Son of the heavenly Father. He never made a mistake with regard to his identity by thinking that he was simply a human being like others. In secret, the Father had given him a special light to enable him to understand that he was truly his Father, in the full meaning of fatherhood. He awakened in him the development of a Son's confidence and got him to call him 'Abba', the family name by which Jewish children called their father. So, through infused knowledge Jesus, from the very beginning, knew that he was the Son of a Father who was God. This was how he became aware of his own divinity, because the fact that the One he called 'Daddy' was his real Father, implied that he, as Son, had the divine nature. In his ceaseless contacts with the Father, his awareness of being the Son of God became ever more clear.

Because of this clarity he discovered the presence of his Father in the Temple. For his pilgrimage to be really true it had to be a pilgrimage to the Father's house. That is what increased his desire to go to Jerusalem each year. For him it was a question of the deepest transport of a Son's heart. His Father's house was his real house, more so than that of Nazareth.

Jesus would not have been able to participate in the paschal meal merely in the same way as the other Passover feast pilgrims. In this domain he had to be in the truth. So he had to discern the essential meaning which this meal had for him. The Father who gave him a unique inner light regarding his identity as Son, also clarified his mission as Son at the same time. He placed him before the perspective of the sacrifice of the paschal lamb, which would win definitive liberation for humanity. He let him catch a glimpse of what the new paschal meal, the eucharistic meal, would be when this liberation had been obtained. So we can conjecture that from a very early age Jesus, when participating in the paschal meal, knew that it was moving towards the Eucharist. He never ate this meal in the perspective of the Jewish tradition only. Because everything he did had to be in truth, thanks to the special light which he received from on high, he always ate it in the most essential truth, that which the symbol was to become.

Consequently, when Jesus desired to go to Jerusalem for the paschal meal, it was with the earnest desire to eat the Passover, but a Passover which for him was a foretaste of the Eucharist. Each time he took part in this meal he must have felt growing in him the aspiration to give to humanity the real spiritual meal which it needed.

Just because we have no direct information about the hidden years at Nazareth, we should not think that they were poor ones for Jesus or that his growth as a child, as an adolescent or as a young man, was just like that of his contemporaries in what concerned his thoughts and feelings. His growth in wisdom and grace before God and people about which Luke speaks (2:25), leads us to suspect a remarkable inner richness in development. The simple word 'Abba', 'Daddy', a word of his very early childhood which remained part of Jesus' language as an adult, would be enough to reveal the hidden wonder of his awareness and the unique way he lived his human existence. From the beginning, Jesus lived out his sonship intensely, and in an exceptionally new way.

That is what is confirmed and manifested in the episode which Luke tells us about.

2. Three days in the Father's house

Jesus reached adolescence at the age of twelve. This is the age at which children begin to move away from their parents and affirm their own personality. Jesus was normally obedient to Joseph and Mary, but here he carried out a symbolic act of emancipation in order to affirm his personality as Son.

He chose the feast of the Passover and the Temple of Jerusalem for this act. By remaining in the Temple for three days he made Mary and Joseph live an inner drama which announced the redemptive mystery. The three days during which he absented himself from his parents' company evoked the three days when he would be taken from his mother by death in order to live in his Father's house.

We can observe the well-thought-out intention which determined his conduct. He deliberately did not tell his parents of his decision to remain in the Temple. We can understand that when he had found his Father's presence in the Temple he wanted to remain there. But what is more surprising is that he was silent about his plan. He knew that by doing this he was going to cause suffering to those who loved him and that they would be looking for him in anguish. His attitude was justified by a higher design. He wanted to associate those who were dearest to him, and especially his mother, with the drama of the cross which was still far away. He, who would later on announce several times to his disciples that the Son of man must die and rise again on the third day, calculated and planned the time span of three days. He knew that his parents would start looking for him on the evening of the first day of the journey, when they realised that he had disappeared, that they would come back to Jerusalem on the second day, and that finally they would find him in the Temple on the third day.

He did not show any regret when Mary asked him, 'Son, why have you treated us so? Behold, your Father and I have been looking for you anxiously'. Apparently he did not allow himself to be troubled because his mother was upset and he replied by asking another question. This was a way of affirming that his conduct was fully justified: 'How is it that you sought me? Did you not know that I must be in my Father's house?' *(Lk 2:48-49)*.

He regretted nothing because he was carrying out the Father's plan by conforming himself to his will. He 'must be' in his Father's house. That must have expressed the need which he would affirm later of the drama of the passion and resurrection. It was a need which came from the Father's sovereignty. It was not because of a whim or a fantasy that he drew his parents into this painful adventure, but because the Father commanded it. We can imagine what it must have cost a twelve-year-old child to make his parents suffer. But he could not hesitate in the face of a command from the Father. He, who would later demand that others sacrifice all human affection in order to be attached to him and follow him, embarked on a way where he sacrificed the deepest affection of a child in order to cling to the Father.

We must add, though, that this episode was not just a painful one. It ended in joy. The more upset his parents were to have lost him, the happier they were to have found him again. In his reply to Mary, Jesus wanted to make her appreciate this movement from suffering to joy. His mother asked him why he had caused them this sadness and she had somewhat revealed the state of her heart when she said to him: 'We have been looking for you anxiously.' When he replied, 'How is it that you sought me?', and by changing the tense of the verb that Mary used, he gave her to understand that she would no longer search for him. She had found him. The reason that he caused her this pain was a mystery indicated by the 'How is it...?' But part of the reason was the consideration that the sadness was destined to turn into joy.

The mystery was that he had to be in his Father's house. Very probably Mary said to him: 'Abba (Daddy) and I have been looking for you'. Jesus replied, 'Did you not know that I must be in Abba's (Daddy's) house?' Mary did not understand. She was speaking about Joseph, but Jesus was speaking about the One whom he had been calling 'Daddy' for a long time, but in the secrecy of his heart. The expression helps us to imagine how happy the twelve-year-old child must have been to stay in his Father's house. He was able to speak to him in a familial way and to express his love as a Son. For him, unlike for the other Jews who came to the Temple, the divine presence was not at all formidable or distant. It had all the warmth of the most tender fatherly presence and gave rise to a dialogue dominated by a single invocation, 'Daddy'.

Having to be in the Father's house meant proclaiming the need to belong totally to the Father and that implied sacrifice. The episode shows that Jesus was committed to this way. In making himself known to Jesus as his real Father, the Father had made him understand that his condition as Son would lead him to a profound sacrifice. His salvific mission was linked to his identity as Son.

In the twelve-year-old Jesus, there appeared the fruit of the whole development of his awareness, thanks to the light given by the Father. He was affirmed in himself as the Son of the Father and he already knew that his attachment to the Father would lead to a drama which would have a happy outcome on the third day.

3. The eucharistic orientation

Is there any sign of a eucharistic perspective in this episode? There is nothing said which would seem to be a reference to the Eucharist. Since the three days were after the celebration of the feast, there is nothing to link them specially to the paschal meal, which had been taken on the eve of the feast.

It remains a fact, nevertheless, that Jesus chose the feast of the Passover to manifest his commitment to the redemptive work and that, because of an illumination given to him by the Father, this feast must have appeared to him as being linked in some way to the·Eucharist. We have already noted that during his annual pilgrimage to Jerusalem Jesus could not have taken part in the paschal meal without thinking of the eucharistic meal which he was going to initiate one day. He saw the paschal meal for what it really was, a figure, a symbolic announcement. It was for him to transform this symbol into a reality.

Now, in order that this transformation could take place, Jesus had to commit himself to the sacrifice in such a way that he was able to give his flesh as food and his blood as drink. It was also necessary for this sacrifice to have glorification as its outcome, since the flesh and blood could have a nutritive value in the spiritual order only if they were in a glorious state filled with the Holy Spirit.

So the paschal meal which Jesus ate when he was twelve years old made him desire the fulfilment of the redemptive sacrifice, which would have its crowning glory in the Father's heavenly house. The three-day episode is to be seen in the context of the prolongation of the basic eucharistic desire. It opened the way for the future institution of the Eucharist even though that was still a long way away. By remaining for three days in the

Father's house after the celebration of the Passover, Jesus symbolically supplied what was lacking in the Passover and preventing it from opening on to the Eucharist.

By this symbolic gesture, he announced the hour 'when he would pass from this world to the Father', when, aware that the Father had given him everything, he would go to him as he had come from him. The words used to describe his attitude at the beginning of the Last Supper (Jn 13:1-3) show the disposition of One who knew that he had to be in his Father's house. It was a eucharistic attitude which he had already adopted at the age of twelve, in the sense that he wanted to express his total belonging to the Father and offer him all that he had received from him.

In the Temple where the Jews came to bless God, to praise him for his favours and to implore his favour for the future, Jesus followed the devotions in a unique way, supplying, by the sincerity and perfection of his disposition, that which had been in the feast of the Passover, which had just taken place. He gave thanks to the Father and offered himself in sacrifice to him, to obtain the salvation of humanity. Because of this, there was a eucharistic dimension to his stay in the Temple.

A certain symbolic announcement of the Eucharist is also sketched under another aspect of this time spent in the Temple. Jesus remained in the Temple in order to prolong the celebration of the Passover feast there. He wanted to remain in the place where he found the continual presence of the Father. He himself prolonged his presence there, united to that of the Father, and let himself be found in the Temple by his parents. We could see in this his intention to prolong a presence; it prefigures the permanent eucharistic presence which will be in the prolongation of the permanent presence of God in the midst of his people in the Holy of Holies.

4. Mary's association with the mystery
Mary is seen as being especially associated with the mystery

represented by the episode. It is true that she shared with Joseph the pain of having lost Jesus and then the joy of finding him. But it was she who was involved in a very special way, because it was she who spoke to Jesus and who received his reply.

What she received above all in this reply was a revelation of the divine identity of her child. By telling her that he 'must be in his Father's house', Jesus indicated that God the Father was his true Father and that he was really the Son of God. Mary had spoken about another 'Daddy', Joseph, and she did not understand. Because of the angel's Annunciation she knew that her child, as the Messiah, was the 'Son of the Most High', and that he was the 'Son of God' because he was conceived of the Holy Spirit (Lk 1:32-35). But the angel had not revealed to her that her child was God the Son, the eternal Son of the Father. And this was the revelation which Jesus made to his mother. He revealed his deepest identity to her. If Mary did not understand at the time, she kept these words in her heart and meditated on them (Lk 2:51) in order to understand their meaning gradually.

At the same time, Jesus revealed to her that there was a painful side to his being the divine Son of the Father. Mary was the one most deeply concerned by the sudden disappearance of her child. Her words to Jesus showed that she had been wronged and that she was hardly able to calm herself even after she had found him. We see in this an affirmation of the intention of the divine plan to associate Mary, in a privileged way, with the redemptive sacrifice.

At first sight, the question, 'Did you not know that I must be in my Father's house?' could seem more surprising. How could Joseph and Mary have known that, since they were so surprised at the way the child behaved? Jesus' words suppose that his parents should have had some indication, which would enable them to understand the meaning of the episode. They made an allusion to the presentation in the Temple, which took place twelve years previously. Joseph and Mary had come to offer the child, but it was Mary who had been specially warned by Simeon's prophecy of what that offering would mean for her; a sword would pierce her soul (Lk 2:35) and in that way she would be associated with the 'contradiction' which her son would experience in his mission as Saviour. That is how Mary was aware, when she offered her son, that she was making the offering for a future sacrifice in which she would participate. She had been the first to offer the redemptive sacrifice. Her offering as a mother came thirty years before Jesus' offering as a priest.

At twelve years of age, Jesus made his mother relive this offering in view of the sacrifice. He remained in the Temple where he had been offered twelve years previously and that was where Mary found him, as a sort of outcome of the gesture of presentation. Now this involvement of Mary in the sacrifice could not be separated from a eucharistic orientation, because this orientation was inscribed in the sacrificial destiny of Jesus. At the presentation in the Temple Mary had made a sacrificial offering which both announced and made possible the future eucharistic offering. We cannot forget, in the eucharistic celebration of the Church, that the sacrifice offered on the altar was first of all formed in Mary's heart when she accepted the piercing by the sword. Mary, who co-operated in a unique way in the redemptive mystery, co-operated in the same way in the advent of the Eucharist.

The discovery of Jesus in the Temple added a symbolic characteristic to this co-operation in the sacrificial aspect. We have noted that by prolonging his stay in his Father's house, Jesus desired to prefigure the prolongation of his eucharistic presence in the continuation of the presence of God in the Temple. When she was searching for her child, Mary was directed towards the Temple as the place where she should find him. She was very surprised to find him in the midst of the doctors. In the Temple the child suddenly revealed what had remained hidden in Nazareth; he revealed his unique personality and began to work wonders. Mary was the first witness of these wonders, which prefigured those which would be accomplished by the eucharistic presence. She was the first to discover a presence which was destined to become a radiating centre and an illumination for a world hungry for truth.

So in Mary we recognise the person who could be said to have introduced the eucharistic mystery. She leads hearts into the eucharistic offering by the very fact that she was the first to commit her heart to the redemptive offering. She leads them to discover the eucharistic presence and the wonders it is destined to produce.

THE THREE PASSOVER FEASTS OF THE PUBLIC LIFE

The gospel of John has preserved for us the memory of the three Passover feasts which marked Jesus' public life. It therefore enables us to determine the length of the public life — two years and some months. Above all, it gives us what we could call the eucharistic structure of the development of Jesus' mission. In fact, according to this gospel, each of the Passover feasts has a eucharistic value. The first two constitute the important landmarks on the way which lead to the institution of the Eucharist and this confirms the strong eucharistic orientation of Jesus' life and shows how it centres on the Passover feasts.

1. The Miracle at Cana, the first announcement of the Eucharist

Jesus' gesture
The miracle at Cana was worked in the perspective of a Passover feast that was close at hand. Actually, shortly afterwards Jesus went to Jerusalem to celebrate the feast: 'The Passover of the Jews was at hand, and Jesus went up to Jerusalem' *(Jn 2:13)*.

It could be said that he wanted to throw light on the meaning of the feast by working a miracle beforehand.

The most immediate objective of the miracle was certainly not to announce the Eucharist. At his mother's request, Jesus wanted to ensure that the wedding feast would be able to continue, by providing plenty of wine. For those present, this miracle revealed publicly and in a very striking way, his power as Saviour. It also stirred up the disciples' faith.

However, there is no doubt about the eucharistic implication of the miracle, even if it was not the primary purpose or the only value of the event. There are many indications of this, all pointing in the same direction.

Jesus wanted to ensure the continuation of the wedding feast. Later on, he himself would use the image of this meal to represent the kingdom of God: 'The kingdom of heaven may be compared to a king who gave a marriage feast for his son' *(Mt 22:2)*. In a certain sense this parable was played out in real life at Cana. The wedding feast had started before Jesus came, but it was thanks to him that it continued, and it was he who symbolically played the role of the spouse who provided wine for his guests. Now we know that, from Jesus' point of view, the heavenly messianic banquet had its earthly prelude in the Eucharist.

So we could affirm that at the beginning of his public life, Jesus wanted to manifest his plan to establish a new meal — a meal of which he would be at the centre: the eucharistic meal which would open out into the heavenly banquet.

Besides, the fact that he gave his own wine is significant. He did not increase, as he could have done, the small amount of wine which may have remained. He gave another wine and in this way witnessed his intention of giving a wine different from all other wines in the meal which he was going to establish. He gave this wine in abundance, because six jars contained a considerable amount. It was far more than was necessary for the feast. Here we have an image of the superabundance of the eucharistic meal, which would be given to us. The jars filled to the brim show that in the Eucharist Christ was going to give the maximum; he could not give more.

As well as that the quality of the wine was remarkable. This did not escape the notice of the master of the feast, who did not know about the miracle but who appreciated the wine which had just been brought him: 'Every man serves the good wine first; and when men have drunk freely, then the poor wine; but you have kept the good wine until now' *(Jn 2:10).* Commentators have been surprised at these words, because there is no record of a custom which consisted in serving the good wine before the less good. It matters little that such a custom has never been mentioned or written down. We know that some people could have behaved in this way. What the reader of the account realises is that the wine which Jesus gave was of a far superior quality. It was a quiet announcement about the quality of the eucharistic wine.

Even the fact that this wine was given to ensure a better ending to the banquet, according to the remark made by the master of the meal, may contain a more profound significance. The good wine is that of the end, the wine which could be called eschatological, the wine which tastes of eternity, because it comes from that eternity. It is the wine of the last times inaugurated by Christ on earth.

What we are doing, above all, is noting the kind of miracle worked by Jesus, a kind that was particularly suited to prefigure the Eucharist. Mary had simply asked her Son to do something about the lack of wine and he could have supplied this wine miraculously in various ways. He chose to change water into wine. This change showed especially his power to transform one material thing into another. It is an announcement of the changing of wine into blood.

Jesus knew that the changing of bread and wine into his body and blood would be a difficult truth to accept as it was so contrary to the ordinary laws of nature. At Cana he gave a demonstration of his omnipotence in this domain by a change which could be proved — the changing of water into wine. The eucharistic transformation or transubstantiation would not be provable. So in his first miracle he gave a visible prelude to it, in order to help faith to be convinced of it.

When we consider the development of the eucharistic structure through the series of Passover feasts, we may wonder why Jesus announced the eucharistic drink first. It was during the second Passover feast that he multiplied the loaves. Now when he promised the Eucharist, he mentioned in the first place the flesh of the Son of man before mentioning his blood, and during the Last Supper he consecrated the bread before he consecrated the cup. So we would have expected that for the long-term preparation for the Eucharist, the miracle of the bread would precede that of the wine. But Jesus followed the reverse order. This order cannot be attributed to chance or to circumstances. The Master carefully chose the miracles he wanted to work and he put the greatest care into the preparation for the institution of the Eucharist. Consequently, he intentionally worked the miracle announcing the eucharistic wine first.

It would seem that his intention was to give a privileged place to the drink, in order to emphasise the spiritual inebriation that he wanted to communicate through the sacrament. There are several aspects to the eucharistic meal. The bread indicates the nourishment which we need each day to live and draws attention to the fact that the Eucharist is not at all a luxury, but food which is necessary for daily Christian life. Wine is a festive drink. It symbolises the feast which every celebration constitutes and it emphasises the effects of joy, ardour and enthusiasm which the sacrament should produce in those who receive it. By choosing first of all to work a miracle, by which he would give miraculous wine, Jesus showed that this aspect of joy and ardour is primordial and cannot be left in the shade. It belongs to the nuptial aspect of the eucharistic banquet; it is the spouse who gives a taste of the sweetness of his love and shares his joy with his guests.

In this way the miracle at Cana invites us to understand better the deep dispositions of Christ's eucharistic heart. This heart is essentially the heart of a spouse. He brought divine love to humanity to the point of sealing a definitive covenant with it. The wine, which he provided miraculously, is the symbol of his love, a love which is given in abundance and which is of the highest quality.

The eucharistic heart is revealed as being particularly attentive to the poor. The poverty of the bride and groom explains the lack of wine. Jesus saved them from the shame of a feast which could have turned into confusion or derision. For these poor people, he ensured the best wine on earth and saved the joy of the wedding feast.

The role of Mary

Since the miracle at Cana had a clear eucharistic thrust, it is worthwhile emphasising Mary's role in the event, to understand her co-operation in the Eucharist better. This role also throws light on a disposition of the Master's eucharistic heart, because it was Jesus whom it pleased to allow and appreciate Mary's intervention in the work of salvation.

We must remember that it was very probably because of his mother that Jesus was at Cana. Mary was not at the wedding simply as a guest. She had come to help in the preparation of the meal and to see that the feast went well. Actually, she was the one who noticed the lack of wine and who tried to remedy the situation. We can understand that Jesus and his disciples had been invited because Mary was there. Perhaps they were passing through Cana at the time, which is what the gospel account suggests: 'There was a marriage at Cana in Galilee, and the mother of Jesus was there; Jesus also was invited to the marriage with his disciples' *(Jn 2:2)*.

So Mary appears as the person who introduces the Eucharist,

as we said previously, when speaking of her role in the presentation of Jesus in the Temple and in the finding of the child when he was twelve years old. It was because of Mary's presence there that Jesus was brought into the wedding feast and made a gesture which announced the Eucharist.

What is highlighted especially by the episode, is Mary's initiative in asking for the miracle. This initiative came from her faith. When she noticed the lack of wine Mary did not try to get some from somewhere close by. She went directly to her Son. By doing that she showed that she believed in his divine power to work miracles. She had never seen Jesus working a miracle. At Nazareth the child had never done such a thing and in his public life Jesus had not yet revealed his power to work miracles. Mary believed in the miracle without ever having seen one. Her faith preceded the miracle, whilst the disciples' faith came after it.

We must note, too, that in requesting the miracle, Mary wanted to bring about the revelation of who her Son really was. She had waited for the moment of this revelation for a long time. The lack of wine was an opportunity to ask her Son for it. Consequently, Mary's request was caused by her desire to co-operate in his work and not just to prolong the wedding feast.

Although she received a reply which did not seem to be too favourable when Jesus reminded her of the distance which had been created between him and her since the beginning of his public life, she did not give up. She understood the difficulty. This wedding feast was not the hour fixed by the Father for the first public revelation. According to the divine plan, the miracle should have taken place later and in other circumstances. We can understand that this plan had foreseen a more important miracle than one giving wine at a festive meal for the first revelation of Jesus' power, but Mary considered that Jesus would be able to overcome that obstacle himself. She believed in his sovereign omnipotence. That is why, gently but firmly, she persevered with her request. She went to the servants to tell them: 'Do whatever he tells you'. She showed that she was expecting a strange order, the order for a miracle, and that the servants would not see the point of it, so she told them to carry it out. By doing this, she let Jesus know that she was counting on a miracle at that time. Her daring perseverance in faith was rewarded. Jesus worked the miracle and revealed himself as she had hoped. The hour which had not yet come had been brought forward and the divine plan was modified to accept Mary's initiative. By working the miracle, Jesus showed publicly his approval of his mother's request. He recognised her mission of collaboration in his work.

The fact that Mary obtained new wine, of better quality and in great abundance, and that she had caused water to be changed into wine by having recourse to her son, suggests the role that was given to her to play at the origin of the Eucharist. If it had not been for her, the first miracle would not have taken place at Cana. She was the reason for the coming of the hour of the miracle which was the first announcement of the Eucharist.

Finally, Mary, who lived through the Cana event so intensely and who marvelled at the working of the miracle, must have meditated very specially on this miracle shortly afterwards, when she was going to Jerusalem for the Passover. Let us recall the words of the gospel text which come after the account of the wedding feast: 'After this he went down to Capharnum with his mother and his brothers and his disciples; and there they stayed for a few days. The Passover of the Jews was at hand, and Jesus went up to Jerusalem' *(Jn 2:12-13)*. Since Mary came back to Capernaum with her Son and since she normally went to Jerusalem for the Passover, she probably went up to Jerusalem with her Son and his disciples. We can imagine that as she was preparing the Passover meal, she was still very struck by the Cana meal. She must have suspected Jesus' intention to transform the sacred meals of Judaism. In particular, the wine served during the paschal meal must have reminded Mary of the better wine which her Son had provided so abundantly at that unforgettable banquet.

Without yet knowing the Eucharist, Mary was deeply committed on the way which led to it. She was hoping for a meal where her Son would give to all people what he had had in view when he changed water into wine and made all the guests appreciate the quality of that wine.

2. The multiplication of the loaves

The miracle

All the evangelists give an account of the miracle of the multiplication of the loaves, but John is the only one who notes the connection of the miracle with the feast of the Passover. He says expressly, 'Now the Passover, the feast of the Jews, was at hand' *(Jn 6:4)*. Once again, Jesus worked the miracle shortly before the feast, as he had done for the wedding feast of Cana. He showed his intention to give a new meaning to that feast. He himself was going to celebrate the feast in a eucharistic perspective and he wanted to associate his disciples with this celebration as seen in a new light.

John writes with solemnity that 'Jesus went up on the mountain and there sat with his disciples' *(Jn 6:3)*. The evangelist wants to emphasise that the Master was in control of the situation. 'Lifting up his eyes, then, and seeing that a multitude was coming to him...', Jesus looked at this hungry multitude. Beyond what he saw close to him, his eyes beheld all the hungry crowds in every part of the world. And what he saw above all, was spiritual hunger. After him, many would concentrate on material hunger to try to remedy it, and the love which Jesus came to spread in the world certainly demands this concern. But he wanted to respond to the most essential human hunger, and in the majestic setting in which he was going to multiply the loaves, his intention was, above all, eucharistic.

He was moved by the situation: 'I have compassion on the

crowd because they have been with me now three days, and have nothing to eat; and I am unwilling to send them away hungry, lest they faint on the way' *(Mt 15:32)*. This compassion reveals the heart of the Saviour. It shows us his compassion for a spiritually hungry humanity, for so many people who, because of lack of food, are in danger of fainting and falling down on the way. It was compassion which characterised his eucharistic heart and was at the origin of the institution of the sacrament.

When the disciples became aware of the situation that Jesus was pointing out to them they saw only one thing that could be done: to send away the crowds so that they themselves could get some food. (Mt 13:15; Mk 6:36). Since the Master refused that, the problem seemed insoluble. To buy loaves? But as Philip observed, 'two hundred denarii would not buy enough bread for each of them to get a little'. To find food among the crowd itself? What could be collected was ridiculously small: Andrew said, 'There is a lad here who has five barley loaves and two fish; but what are they among so many?' *(Jn 6:7-9)*. There was no human solution possible.

Christ was the only one who was able to give the crowd its true food. He had foreseen everything. He had chosen a place where there was plenty of grass and where it was easy to seat the five thousand around him. This choice was a prelude to his later one of the room for the celebration of the Last Supper, a meal whose smallest details he had foreseen. Here he told his disciples to organise the meal. 'Make them sit down in companies, about fifty each' *(Lk 9:14)*. There is a parallel here with the instructions which he would give to the disciples whom he put in charge of the last paschal meal.

Here we must note the role which was expressly given to the disciples. When they had proposed that the crowds be sent away and so rid themselves of the problem, he made them feel their responsibility: 'You give them something to eat' *(Mt 14:16; Mk 6:37; Lk 9:13)*. This collaboration, which was so clearly required, makes us think of the Eucharist. At the wedding feast of Cana,

Mary's co-operation was shown in the obtaining of the miracle. Here it is the co-operation of the apostles, but it took another form. Unlike Mary, they did not ask for a miracle. They would even have wished to avoid one by looking for a human solution to the problem and by dismissing the crowds. But in a way, Jesus asked them to be the instruments of the miracle by being involved in the distribution of the loaves. He wanted them to be his ministers, as it were, in this meal which announced the Eucharist.

He used five loaves and two fish to work the miracle. This seemed ridiculous, but Jesus despised nothing and wanted the miraculous meal to start from the small amount of provisions which they had.

The basis for the spiritual food of the Eucharist would be the humble daily bread, which is such a small thing in comparison with the Saviour's body, but which shows the contribution of the work of human hands to the offering of the Eucharist, to the gift which the participants make of the little that they have, so that it can be transformed into the richness of Christ.

When he took the loaves, Jesus raised his eyes to heaven. According to the synoptics he said a prayer of blessing; according to the johannine account, it was a prayer of thanksgiving. We must note, however, that in his second account of the multiplication of the loaves, Matthew no longer speaks of blessing but of thanksgiving (15:36). We have remarked that the verb 'to bless', interpreted Jesus' prayer according to Jewish tradition, while the verb 'to give thanks' recognised the newness which was going to characterise the Eucharist.

The action of 'breaking the bread' before distributing it is also characteristic, because in the primitive Church the eucharistic celebration would be called 'the breaking of the bread'. The disciples received the bread and gave it to the crowd. They did the same with the fish.

No less significant is the abundance of the food given by Jesus which presaged the abundance of the eucharistic meal; 'And they all ate and were satisfied' *(Mk 6:42)*. They received 'as much as they wanted' *(Jn 6:11)*. This abundance was not to go to waste. It showed divine generosity, but did not mean that what was given in abundance would have less value. 'Gather up the fragments left over, that nothing may be lost', Jesus said *(Jn 6:12)*. The concern that nothing might be lost would remain a dominant one in the Eucharist, whose fruitfulness should be as great as possible. The twelve baskets filled with fragments testify both to the super-abundance of the meal and to the preoccupation not to allow anything to be lost which could satisfy human hunger.

Why did Jesus want to multiply the fish at the same time as the loaves? Later on, the fish would come to be regarded as a symbol of Christ, because of the fact that the Greek word contains the initials of his identity: 'Jesus Christ, Son of the Saving God' *(ichtus)*. This could not have been the symbolism involved here. It looks as if Jesus wanted to show his intention to give a complete meal to the crowd by adding the fish to the loaves. In this way he announced his will to make of the Eucharist the most complete spiritual meal. By completely satisfying the hungry crowd, he wanted to give all human crowds what they would need to start out again and not faint on the way.

The reaction to the miracle

As soon as the miracle had been worked, it was interpreted by the crowd as a first step towards the messianic kingdom: 'When the people saw the sign which he had done they said, 'This is indeed the prophet who is to come into the world!' *(Jn 6:14)*. Those who had been filled recognised him as the Messiah according to their hopes of a messianic kingdom where an abundance of material goods would reign. The One who had just given them bread at will seemed to be the ideal Messiah, the King who could freely nourish the inhabitants of his kingdom.

This was not the image which Jesus wished to give of himself, nor was it the true meaning of the miracle: 'Perceiving then that they were about to come and take him by force to make him king, Jesus withdrew again to the mountain by himself' *(Jn 6:15)*. He did not want any part in the attempts to set him on the way to being a political Messiah. Before sending away the crowds and withdrawing to the mountain, he made the disciples get into a boat and go before him to the other side of Bethsaida (Mk 6:45). The fact that he had to make the disciples do this shows that they shared the enthusiasm of the crowd. They saw it as the opportunity they had dreamed of, to launch themselves into the people's messianic adventure. Jesus made them give up their dream for the moment.

In fact, while it appeared to be a great success, the multiplication of the loaves immediately placed Jesus in a very embarrassing situation. Neither the crowd nor the disciples were able to understand the true meaning of the miracle. They interpreted it in a political way, which the Master wanted to refute resolutely. Jesus was able to foresee the struggle he would have to make the hidden purpose of the miracle known and accepted. He certainly had not achieved his objective by feeding the crowd, because contrary to what many may have thought, he had not come to put an end to material hunger in the world. His aim was much higher, and that was where he met the obstacle. He would have to discourage all the false hopes that had resulted from his compassionate gesture.

He gave himself to prayer to overcome the obstacle. John emphasises that he went away alone to the mountain, and Matthew also insists on this solitude (14:23). Jesus wanted to go before the Father to entrust to him this situation where he felt isolated and alone against everyone. The contrast, between the wave of enthusiasm which swept through the crowd and the solitary dialogue which he had with his Father, is very striking. He distanced himself from false hopes in order to enter into the truth of the real hope of the miracle.

This truth was the Eucharist which was to come. The miracle had no meaning apart from that, and Jesus was going to have to show it because he could no longer content himself, as he did at Cana, with a miracle whose symbolism remained unexplained. This was the second Passover feast, half-way through the public life. The institution of the Eucharist had to be prepared for now, so that it would be better understood and accepted when it took place. That was why the real meaning of the multiplication of the loaves had to be explained. But it could be foreseen that the explanation would offend, either because of indifference or because of a strong resistance on the part of those who wanted a temporal messianism.

The long nocturnal prayer came from the eucharistic heart of Jesus and ended at the fourth watch, just before dawn. This prayer was actually animated by the desire to announce clearly the great plan of the Eucharist in emphasising the favours it would bring. Jesus had waited for this moment for a long time. Now the circumstances seemed very favourable, and the result of this announcement had, more than ever, to be entrusted to the Father.

While Jesus prayed in solitude, the disciples must have been struggling against strong waves. In spite of appearances the Master did not abandon them: 'He saw that they were making headway painfully, for the wind was against them', says Mark *(6:48)*. He saw them from a higher plane. But he saw, above all, the most formidable difficulty, that of their hopes for a messianic kingdom of this world, which would turn them away from the more spiritual perspective of the Eucharist. If Jesus, by his prayer, supported the courage of his disciples on the agitated waters of the lake, he wanted, above all, to affirm them in the struggle which they would have the following day against the violent wind of desertion.

Jesus wished to obtain for them by his prayer the grace to hold on to the promise of the Eucharist. He had hardly any hope of making the crowd understand this announcement. Jesus regretted that 'everything was in parables' for them and on this occasion this meant that they saw the multiplication of the loaves only as something material. But the gate of the mystery had been opened for the apostles to whom 'the mystery of the kingdom of God had been given' *(Mk 4:11)*, so that they could believe in the Eucharist.

By rejoining his disciples at the end of the night by walking on the water, Jesus showed his eagerness to come to their aid for a day which was going to be turbulent.

The first eucharistic teaching

In the synagogue at Capernaum, the Master commented on the previous evening's miracle and gave his first eucharistic teaching. It was a great discourse which was developed in dialogue and about which there was much talk.

Some have seen two distinct parts in this discourse — the first about faith, and the second treating of the Eucharist. In fact the whole discourse is about the Eucharist. From the beginning Jesus spoke about 'the food which endures to eternal life' *(Jn 6:27)* and the bread from heaven which the Father gives (Jn 6:32-33). Afterwards, in certain replies, he insisted very much on faith, but he did this precisely to obtain faith in the Eucharist.

Our aim is not to analyse the development of this discourse. We have already commented on some of its affirmations. What remains to be done is to highlight briefly the parts of it which flow most clearly from the eucharistic heart of the Master. In this discourse, which he had been waiting for so long to give, we find not only a doctrine proclaimed forcefully, but also the expression of his deepest attitudes of mind and heart, and his most lively feelings.

First of all, Jesus indicated that the primary author of the Eucharist was the Father. It was he who had sent his Son into the world marking him with his seal, and it was he who gave the bread from heaven. It was to his will that Jesus was conformed (Jn 6:38). So when he proposed the Eucharist, he had the guarantee that he was carrying out the Father's will. In fact it was this guarantee which would make him steadfast in the crisis caused by his words. He did what the Father wanted with a perseverance which no opposition could discourage.

Besides, it was on the Father that he depended for the efficacy of his teaching. When he heard the murmuring against his words, he declared that assent to his doctrine could only come from being drawn by the Father: 'No one can come to me unless the Father who sent me draws him' *(Jn 6:44)*. Had he not prayed to the Father for a whole night that his disciples at least would experience this attraction and would not resist it?

If the first cry of Christ's heart was the Father, we can also see a particular thrust in the affirmations, 'I am the bread of life' *(Jn 6:34-48)* and 'I am the living bread come down from heaven' *(Jn 6:51;* cf 6:41-58). The fact that he repeated these affirmations several times shows how much he insisted on them. Jesus presented himself as people's spiritual food. It was he, it was his person, that he was giving as food by means of his body and blood. After having said 'He who eats my flesh and drinks my blood' *(Jn 6:56)* he said, meaning the same thing, 'he who eats me' *(Jn 6:57)*. He wanted to show that he was not just giving something of himself in the Eucharist, but the whole of himself, everything that he was. He repeated that he was the bread of life, with an ardour which drove him to hand himself over unreservedly to humanity and to enter into the depths of human life to make it blossom. Allowing themselves to be eaten by others is a beautiful image to show the devotion of those who forget themselves in order to serve. In Jesus the image became a reality. Not only does he allow himself to be eaten, but he does so in order to become the life of the person who takes him as food.

By that very fact, we can understand the capital importance of the Eucharist. It is in this sacrament that we find the most complete giving of the person of Christ, with his deepest action on human life. He makes himself present in order to pour out his divine life.

No less striking is the physical realism of a spiritual meal: 'Truly, truly, I say to you, unless you eat the flesh of the Son of man and drink his blood, you have no life in you' *(Jn 6:53)*. To those who might be tempted to object, he declared immediately: 'For my flesh is food indeed, and my blood is drink indeed' *(Jn 6:55)*.

The vigour with which he made these affirmations came from his desire to present the Eucharist as the utmost point of the mystery of the incarnation. The human flesh which he, the Son of God, had taken on to come among us, would never cease to be present on earth. It would completely fulfil its function as the flesh of the Saviour by nourishing humanity for ever. For him, flesh and blood were not simply a passing earthly condition. They would remain, not only in a glorious state in heaven, but in the obscurity of the life of the Church on earth.

Finally, in the announcement of the Eucharist, a very strong accent was placed on its importance for eternal life and the resurrection. To those who remembered the manna as the supreme food, Jesus did not hesitate to declare that 'Your fathers ate the manna in the wilderness and they died. This is the bread which comes down from heaven, that a man may eat it and not die' *(Jn 6:49-50)*. The big problem was that of obtaining a life which would not be subject to death. This is the problem to which the Eucharist responds in a decisive manner: 'He who eats my flesh and drinks my blood has eternal life, and I will raise him up on the last day' *(Jn 6:54)*.

There are two aspects to victory over death. The flesh and blood of the Son of man obtain first of all eternal life, in such a way that it becomes a present possession. It is not just a question of the life that we will enjoy after death, but an eternal life which begins during our earthly existence. This life will continue into the beyond and as well as that at the end of the world it will be accompanied by a resurrection wrought by

Christ. The flesh of Christ, by nourishing the human being, brings to the flesh a guarantee of a blessed resurrection.

Through the Eucharist, Jesus wanted to communicate the eternity which he possessed in himself by handing over his divine life.

The great trial

The announcement of the Eucharist should have given rise to great enthusiasm. It was the announcement of the greatest wonder which Jesus could offer to people for the development of their spiritual life. In fact, among a good number of the disciples, it caused immense disappointment.

Of course we cannot be surprised at the discussions which the discourse could have caused among those who did not believe in Jesus. But what was more serious was the reaction of the disciples, that is to say, of those who had followed Jesus until then and had faith in him.

John states clearly that the opposition came from them: 'Many of his disciples, when they heard it, said, "This is a hard saying; who can listen to it?"' Then Jesus gave an explanation to dispel a misunderstanding: the body and blood of the Son of God should be given as food and drink, not in their earthly state, but in the glorious state of the ascension, where the Son of God would have ascended 'where he was before'. In this state the flesh and blood would be filled with the Holy Spirit (Jn 6:61-63).

When he had given that clarification, he emphasised that the essential problem of his listeners with regard to the announcement which he had just made was one of faith. 'But there are some of you that do not believe' *(Jn 6:64)*. Once he had explained his doctrine well, he could not but ask for faith. And here we have the drama: 'After this many of his disciples drew back and no longer went about with him' *(Jn 6:66)*. It was after the discourse which gave the most promise for the future and which was the most enriching for the life of the community, that defections suddenly multiplied. Jesus literally saw the group of his faithful ones dissolving.

Never again was he to experience this kind of trial. The desertion of a great number, before his very eyes, must have caused him deep sorrow. We could say that at that moment his eucharistic heart was pierced by the sword of incredulity.

However the twelve still remained close to him. That was his last hope. Was he going to do something special to invite them to remain with him? Far from encouraging them warmly to remain with him, he asked them a question: 'Do you also wish to go away?' *(Jn 6:67)*. That meant that if the twelve had the same dispositions as the many disciples who had abandoned him, they should also leave. It placed them in a dilemma. Either they had to believe in the Eucharist or go away. Jesus did not compromise on the necessity for faith in the Eucharist. He was ready to risk losing the apostolic community which he had formed around him, if they did not believe in what he had come to proclaim.

Of course, with his whole heart he desired that the twelve would be faithful. The whole of the previous night he had prayed to the Father in order to obtain for them the necessary light and strength to keep the faith. But he did not try in any way to make their assent easier. He clearly left the responsibility of their option to his apostles. They had to make the choice in complete freedom.

The first words of Peter's reply contained a beautiful expression of personal attachment: 'Lord, to whom shall we go?' However, they seem to reflect a previous hesitation. The apostle who had seen so many defections around him had been tempted to leave. But where could he go? Only the Lord could give meaning to his life.

Peter made a profession of faith which did not directly mention the promised Eucharist, but which showed a general belief in all that Jesus had taught: 'You have the words of eternal life; and we have believed, and have come to know, that you are the Holy One of God' *(Jn 6:69)*. Even if the Master's words had taken him by surprise, or had caused him a certain repugnance, he had overcome that because of his attachment to Christ.

Jesus' prayer was answered. Peter's declaration gave immense joy to the Master. The first eucharistic teaching gained a firm adherence of faith from those who, later on, would receive the mission of celebrating the Eucharist in memory of the Lord.

Judas was the only one who did not share in this faith. He had been more disappointed than the others by Jesus' discourse. The miracle of the multiplication of the loaves had given him the hope of an abundance of material goods and now he had to give that up. Since he did not believe when the Eucharist was announced, he would have left if he had been loyal. It was hypocritical of him to stay, and that was why Jesus said: 'One of you is a devil' *(Jn 6:70)*. We can guess the secret pain this attitude caused the Master. Judas betrayed the Eucharist before he betrayed Jesus himself.

However, the betrayal, with the pain it caused, could not negate the essential result which had been achieved: the first witness of the faith of the early Church in the Eucharist.

3. The Last Supper

The paschal meal
Some exegetes have doubted that the Last Supper was a paschal meal. These doubts come especially from the chronology given in John's gospel. According to this chronology, Jesus was crucified on the eve of the Passover at the hour when the paschal lamb was being slain. That meant that he died before the paschal meal, which was eaten on the evening of the vigil of the feast. The conclusion was that the Last Supper, which was eaten on the evening of the day before the paschal vigil, could not have been the paschal meal.

The chronological exactitude of John must be accepted. It

corresponds with certain details of the trial, especially with the fact that Jesus' accusers did not enter Pilate's praetorium 'so that they might not be defiled, and might eat the Passover' *(Jn 18:28)*. It also explains the great activity surrounding the condemnation of Jesus which would have been unthinkable if Jesus had been crucified on the day of the Passover itself. The Jews, who wanted to have finished with him, organised a trial quickly, so that everything could be over before the feast. The same haste with regard to the burial of Jesus, whose body was placed in a tomb close by, can be explained by the closeness of the feast. Many things mentioned in the gospel, such as the meeting with Simon of Cyrene, who was coming back from the fields in the middle of the day, as was the custom on the eve of the Passover, confirm this chronological datum.

So Jesus was put to death on the eve of the Passover, even more precisely, on the eve of a Passover feast which that year coincided with the Sabbath, so that the Sabbath was a high day (Jn 19:31). However this dating is not a reason for discarding the very clear affirmation of the synoptics: the meal which Jesus had with his apostles on the eve of his death was a paschal meal. According to Mark's account the apostles were expecting a paschal meal, because they asked the Master: 'Where will you have us go and prepare for you to eat the Passover?' When Jesus sent his two disciples he gave them directions, which show just as clearly his intention to eat the paschal meal: 'Go into the city and a man carrying a jar of water will meet you; follow him and wherever he enters, say to the householder, "The teacher says, Where is my guest room, where am I to eat the Passover with my disciples?" And he will show you a large upper room furnished and ready; there prepare for us'. The evangelist adds that they found it as he had told them and that 'they prepared the Passover' *(Mk 14:12-16)*. So he could not have had any doubt about the nature of the meal; it was a paschal meal.

As well as that, the two consecratory prayers over the bread and over the cup are inserted into the rites of the paschal meal.

And many other points could be taken, which show the paschal character of the Last Supper.[12]

How can it be explained why Jesus wanted to have a paschal meal the day before the eve of the Passover? This must certainly have been tolerated, at least by custom. It would seem that the most probable reason was a difference of date for the feast of the Passover between the Galileans and the Judeans. It was by observing the moon that the exact date of the Passover feast was fixed each year. Sometimes in Galilee the new moon was observed a day earlier than in Judaea and the year 30, in which the death of Jesus took place, was a year in which this difference was possible. We could then consider that the Galileans who had come to Jerusalem would have the paschal meal on the eve of the day on which it was organised for the inhabitants of Judaea.[13]

So that is the explanation of how Jesus was easily able to find a room ready for the paschal meal. The owner of the room would only be using it the following day for his family's paschal meal. Jesus and his disciples could therefore use it without causing any inconvenience, the day before the eve of the official Passover feast.

The new paschal meal
The detail with which Jesus gave instructions to his disciples about the preparation of the paschal meal, shows the care with which he would have foreseen every detail of what would happen during the meal.

We have already commented on various aspects of the institution of the Eucharist and emphasised how he retained two essential rites from the paschal meal and gave them a new meaning by consecrating the bread and wine. By the words 'Do this in remembrance of me', which marked the two rites, Jesus

12. cf Jeremias *La dernière cène*, 42-66.
13. cf S. Dockx, OP., *Chronologies néotestamentaires et Vie de l'Église primitive. Recherches exégétiques*, Paris-Gembloux 1976, 21-29.

showed that he was founding a new paschal meal. Until then, the paschal meal was eaten in memory of Yahweh, who had delivered the Jewish people from the Egyptian yoke. From now on, it would be eaten in remembrance of Jesus, whose sacrifice brought true freedom to humanity. Christ placed himself at the centre of the liturgy of his Church.

This newness was surprising, but the disciples were prepared to accept it. By the profession of faith, which Jesus had asked of them beforehand on the road to Caesarea Philippi, they had recognised in Jesus the Messiah and Son of God, the centre of the new faith. So they were able to understand as well, that from now on, the most important liturgical rite would be carried out in remembrance of Jesus, the Saviour of humanity.

The words, 'This is my flesh', 'This is my blood, the blood of the covenant', which brought out the newness of the meal even more, could have seemed to be simple metaphorical statements, if the disciples had not already had to express their faith in the announcement that the flesh and blood of the Son of man would be given as food and drink. What had been promised by Jesus after the multiplication of the loaves was now accomplished. The disciples, who had had the time to deepen within themselves the profession of faith which Peter made during the eucharistic 'crisis', were not taken unawares by the amazing statements of the Master. They were able to accept them for what they really meant and to integrate them deeply into their faith.

The statements 'This is my flesh', 'This is my blood' were very surprising, because they expressed a divine commitment in the new paschal meal which was much more radical than Yahweh's commitment in the Jewish people's paschal meal. The Son of God committed himself to the point of becoming food and drink. From this point of view alone, it could be understood why the rest of the old paschal meal was destined to disappear. How could other food and drink be kept when the new meal gave divine food and divine drink? Nothing of the paschal lamb or of what went with it could remain, because it was God alone in Christ who had to nourish and quench people's thirst.

The divine commitment showed its generosity in the sacrifice. For Jesus, the first announcement of the Eucharist had been a trial. It had cost him deep moral suffering, because of the bad reception which so many disciples gave to a promise he made with so much love. In that, there was a sign of the sacrifice which the Eucharist itself involved. During the Last Supper, the Master had the joy of seeing that the disciples received with faith what he was offering them, with the exception of Judas, who was plunging into his betrayal. But he had to face another trial which was very close: the Passion, and he committed himself to the sacrifice, by distributing his body, which was going to be given up, and his blood, which was going to be shed for the human race.

The third paschal meal of his public life was inseparable from the third Passover feast, when the drama of the cross took place. That was the way it brought about the total opening of the eucharistic heart of Jesus.

5

Fundamental eucharistic aspirations

After having followed the development of the eucharistic dispositions of Jesus and the gradual preparation for the institution of the Eucharist, it now remains for us to treat of some fundamental aspirations which result from the Master's words and enable us to discover his eucharistic heart better. These aspirations can be seen especially during the Last Supper.

THE WILL TO BE PRESENT CONTINUALLY

1. 'I am the vine.'

Among the words said as a commentary during the first eucharistic meal, we find the statement, 'I am the true vine' *(Jn 15:1)*. We understand that this image of the vine would have been used in connection with the cup which Jesus consecrated for his disciples. Under the appearance of wine, he gave them his blood to drink. He wanted to explain more about the symbolism of wine, whose red colour was especially suited to evoke blood. It was a symbol which was based, not only on a superficial resemblance, but on a deep reality. The One who was giving the wine was himself the vine.

In that way, Jesus let it be known that he was not content just to give at certain times the wine, which would inebriate his disciples spiritually. He is the One who gives the spiritual drink permanently and who wishes to remain a continual source of life.

When he presented himself as the vine, Jesus went beyond the statements that he had made about his personal presence in the Eucharist. During the first announcement of the Eucharist, as we have already emphasised, he said about himself: 'I am the bread of life' (Jn 6:35-48). He is the bread just as he is the wine, because the presence of his flesh and blood signifies the presence of his person. To eat his flesh and to drink his blood means eating and drinking himself. But when he said that he was the vine, he was not simply referring to the passing act of the eucharistic meal. He was claiming a presence in every moment of his disciples' lives, a presence by which he communicated to them his own life, which would become theirs and which would ensure fruitfulness.

He insisted on their need to abide in him as he abided in them, and also on the fruits which depended on that vital link: 'I am the vine, you are the branches. He who abides in me, and I in him, he it is that bears much fruit, for apart from me you can do nothing' (Jn 15:5). The disciples were no longer just those who became inebriated with the fruit of his vine. They were the branches of the vine, the branches which had to receive the sap from him in order to bear fruit.

The aim of the Eucharist was to ensure more and more that fundamental link with Christ. It helped the disciples to be nourished by the life of Christ and to receive their spiritual life more and more abundantly from him. To follow through the images already used, the more the blood of Christ is taken as wine which inebriates the soul, the more he can be the vine which continually gives its sap — his divine life.

The eucharistic meal aims at developing the most intimate union with the Saviour through a mutual belonging which is prolonged indefinitely. 'Abide in me and I in you' (Jn 15:4). This word 'abide' expresses Jesus' most profound aspiration at this last meal. He repeated it insistently. The branch must 'abide in the vine', be joined with it, and in the same way, the disciples should remain attached to Christ and be linked up to his love: 'Abide in my love' *(Jn 15:9)*.

Jesus was about to end his earthly life and he wanted nothing of what he had brought into the world to be lost. He was not content just to announce to his disciples that he would see them after a while. His resurrection would enable him to meet them soon again, on the third day, as he always said when he announced his death as though he wanted, each time, to insist on the shortness of his absence. He wanted to stay with them for a longer period than the time he would be with them after he had risen, to be permanently present in the very depths of people's beings, in order to guarantee a constant communication of life to his faithful.

By declaring that apart from him they could be nothing, and that whoever abided in him would bear much fruit, he was thinking, above all, of spiritual fruitfulness. He was thinking of the mission entrusted to his disciples, a mission which was so important for the development of the Church. They could carry out this mission only in so far as they remained united to him, or abided in him. Apostolic action cannot hope for fruitfulness if it is not based on deep intimacy with the Lord.

However, he was not thinking just of the fruits of apostolic action. The image used, that of the vine and the branches, shows clearly that the personal life of the disciples could only mature through attachment to Christ. The branch receives all its life from the vine and that enables it to bear fruit. As soon as it becomes separated, not only does it become sterile, but it dies: it dries up and is good for nothing except to be thrown on the fire (Jn 15:6).

So, in the Eucharist, Christ always presents himself as the vine. He invites Christians to be like the branch, eager for abundant life and great fruitfulness. He is continually trying to renew a presence which he desires to be permanent within the soul. By coming into those who eat and drink him, he desires to abide in them in such a way that they can abide in him and remain in contact with the source of life.

2. 'I am with you'

According to Matthew's Gospel, Jesus' last words to his apostles before going to heaven were a promise of perpetual presence: 'I am with you always, to the close of the age' *(Mt 28:20)*.

He could not have made a more characteristic declaration on his departure. Jesus was going to accompany the disciples and the whole Church on their journey to the close of the age. He was disappearing only in order to remain on earth in another way. Here we find again his intention 'to abide', which was so vividly expressed during the Last Supper.

We should, however, note a difference of emphasis. In the exhortation, 'Abide in me and I in you', he was thinking of a permanent presence in the human being, which would communicate life within. In the promise, 'I am with you', it is more a question of a presence which establishes relationships with people, which accompanies them in order to help them. The invitation 'to abide' during the Last Supper, concerns especially the transformation of human nature by means of an infusion of divine life, while the guarantee given by the risen Christ had more to do with personal relationships — it refers to a presence which acts more from the outside.

The words 'I am with you' express, first of all, the divine 'I am' of Jesus. Jesus applied the divine name of Yahweh to himself several times. Sometimes the allusion was clear, like in the declaration, 'Before Abraham was, I am' *(Jn 8:58)*. By claiming this name for himself, Jesus did not want only to affirm his absolute and eternal existence as God, but his definitive presence on earth. In Exodus (3:14) the revelation of the name of Yahweh, 'I am', had shown the unshakeable power of the divine presence. Through his human life on earth, Jesus became this presence in a very real way. And this divine presence of the Word who lived among people was not going to be lost. At the time of his trial before the Sanhedrin, Jesus replied to Caiphas' decisive question by affirming an 'I am' which attested to his divine identity and which also showed his certainty of a presence which would triumph over death (Mk 14:62; Lk 22:70). When he appeared to his disciples after his resurrection he had confirmed this 'I am', which, from then on, would possess a human life, which nothing could extinguish *(Lk 24:39)*. Shortly before leaving his disciples to go to heaven, he repeated the declaration 'I am' to affirm a presence which would guide their whole future.

This time he gave the meaning of the presence more clearly. It was not a solitary presence, but one of being in the company of his disciples. Besides, when he said, 'I am with you', he was taking up the original intention of God in the 'I am' revelation. God had unveiled his name to Moses as a guarantee of the covenant, 'I will be with you' *(Ex 3:12)*. Jesus also wanted to express the covenant, the covenant which was made after his sacrifice.

In order to emphasise the strength of the covenant, he used a forceful expression which should be translated literally: 'I — with you — am'. The words 'with you' were inserted into the 'I am', as if to show that, from then on, they would be inseparable. The covenant with us was inserted into the very name of God. This covenant would be indissolubly bound to the divine presence.

We can guess the aspirations of Christ's heart in the desire to remain with his disciples indefinitely. He had wanted to be with them so much during his earthly life that he wanted to be in their company throughout history. He showed, more especially, his desire to be with them 'all days'. He wanted to be present in the least instant of every human existence. No moment, however brief, could be deprived of his presence.

Besides, the declaration came from the eucharistic heart of the Master. 'I will be with you', meant the presence of Christ in the most general way, without specifying the forms of that presence. In reality, it could be applied to all modes of presence whatever they might be. There is a multiplicity of forms of the Lord's presence, which bears witness to the richness of his personal gift to humanity. But among these there is one which has the greatest substance — the eucharistic presence. It would have been surprising if Jesus was not thinking of the sacramental presence which he intended to offer to his Church when he stated his intention to be present continually. This presence prolongs the mystery of the incarnation in the most definite way, because it hands over the person of Christ in his flesh and blood.

More especially, Jesus must have had the aspiration to establish the perpetual eucharistic presence. He desired to fulfil to the maximum what had been prefigured in the old covenant. Yahweh wanted to abide in the midst of his people, in a place where his presence would be recognised and venerated. During the Exodus, he abided in the meeting tent, a tent pitched outside the camp, which signified, at one and the same time, an abiding in the manner of people, and an abiding apart. This was the tent to which Moses went to consult God: 'Thus the Lord used to speak to Moses face to face, as a man speaks to his friend' *(Ex 33:11)*, and when Moses came out of the tent, 'the people of Israel saw... that the skin of Moses' face shone'. Afterwards, when the Temple of Jerusalem was built, the divine presence was localised in the Holy of Holies, where the ark of the covenant had been placed.

Jesus could not be less generous in the gift of his presence. If he had not given his Church a permanent presence with a definite localisation, the new covenant would have been inferior to the old one in that respect. Now he wanted to fulfil completely all that had been announced in a symbolic way in the Jewish tradition. Therefore he ensured that the Christian community would have a perpetual presence, with the fullness which characterised the fulfilling of promises. He gave a sacramental presence which, because of its physical reality, was superior to Yahweh's presence in the Temple, and a presence which was not limited to a single place as it was in Judaism, but which extended to a multitude of places in order to be more widely available to all.

He did not formulate the doctrine of this permanent eucharistic presence with precision, but, as in many other domains, he gave us indicative clues. When he instituted the Eucharist, he was not content just to give his flesh to be eaten and his blood to be drunk. He declared: 'This is my flesh', 'This is my blood'. In this way, he affirmed above all the presence of his flesh and blood and he did not give any time limit for it. He showed his intention to place the emphasis on the gift of his presence. Besides, when he declared, 'This is my blood, the blood of the covenant', he was alluding to the covenant made with Moses during the Exodus (Ex 24:8). Now it was this covenant which included the continual presence of God in the midst of his people, localised in the meeting tent where Moses could speak with God face to face. Jesus would not have wanted a covenant of lesser quality. Therefore he had to establish a covenant through his blood, which would enable his disciples to have the face-to-face meetings which Moses had, thanks to a permanent presence. He was the first to desire such intimate meetings in the same climate of friendship, and he wanted his disciples' faces also to shine after the meetings.

And so it was that he wanted to foster the development of contemplation in Christian piety. This contemplation is an essential way of being attached to his person. In his revelation, Jesus first of all unveiled what he was: the Christian religion is the religion of a person, the Son of God made man, who is the primary object of faith. The repeated statements, 'I am', or 'It is I', draw attention to his personal identity.

The 'I am with you all days', makes us understand that the 'I am' is a call to a meeting, to a reunion. Jesus offers himself continually to our gaze and for dialogue. The importance which he attached to this intimate contact appears in his reply to Martha, when he showed her that her sister Mary was right to sit at his feet to listen to his word. Only one thing was needed and 'Mary has chosen the good portion, which shall not be taken from her' *(Lk 10:42)*. While appreciating Martha's devotedness, he underlined the priority of affective attachment to his person. Jesus never ceases to offer the better portion of human existence to those who allow themselves to be drawn by the permanent eucharistic presence. He offers them access to peaceful and silent contemplation.

On the other hand, the guarantee of the 'I am with you', has the aim of helping in all the disciples' activities. The words 'to the end of the age' indicate the length of time it will take for the Church to reach full development on earth, because the end will come when all nations have been evangelised (Mt 24:14). Jesus wanted to give support to this development by his presence. He would be with his disciples in the whole accomplishment of their mission and in their witnessing. In this way, the permanent eucharistic presence is the sign of Christ's commitment in the development of the life of the Christian community, of its expansion and in all the events of each disciple's life.

In this way, the eucharistic presence has a dynamic character. The eucharistic Christ wants to be present to all his faithful, to make their faces radiant, to support and encourage them in their difficulties and to press them forward to proclaim the gospel to the universe. The eucharistic heart of Jesus seeks contemplatives in order to make missionaries of them.

THE DESIRE FOR UNITY OF LOVE

1. Humble service, the solution to quarrels

The problem of unity was posed in a vivid and immediate way during the Last Supper, since at the beginning of the meal the disciples quarrelled about which of them was the greatest (Lk 22:24). Was it a quarrel about places at the table? We do not know. But the cause of the quarrel was nothing new. It was the clash of the ambitions of those who coveted the first place in the kingdom which Jesus was going to inaugurate.

This dispute on the threshold of the Eucharist has a symbolic value. It evokes all the conflicts which would exist among Christians and even among pastors, when the horizon of the kingdom would be regarded with purely human eyes. But it also has the advantage of highlighting the remedy which the Master proposed. It directs our attention towards the Eucharist which offers the essential response to the problems posed by dissension.

Not only did Jesus say that the greatest should be the one who served, but he showed it by his own actions. He washed his disciples' feet. Washing guests' feet before the meal was a servant's work. As a child in the home at Nazareth Jesus would have seen his mother doing it and then, when he was older, he would have followed her example and done it himself. In this instance, he did it with the full awareness of his sovereignty as the Son who had received everything from the Father (Jn 13:3). Peter, who beforehand had proclaimed his faith in Jesus the Messiah and Son of God so openly, found this action unworthy of the One who was Lord. By this he showed that he had not yet understood the humble service which animated his Master's whole mission. But his opposition had to give way before the firm request of Jesus, who asked him to accept the mystery: 'What I am doing, you do not know now, but afterward you will understand' (Jn 13:7).

The lesson was as clear as the action: 'If I then, your Lord and Teacher, have washed your feet, you also ought to wash one another's feet' (Jn 13:14). That is the solution to all quarrels caused by ambition. If a person, instead of setting himself up as the greatest, becomes the smallest, and takes on the role of a servant, all disputes over having the first place will disappear. Because the One who possessed divine greatness washed his disciples' feet, none of them could try any longer to place himself on a higher level. There is only one legitimate way, that of the most humble service.

This service, rendered at the time when Jesus knew the hour had come for him to go to the Father (Jn 13:1), implies that he was committed to the redemptive sacrifice. The Master had shown the final direction of his service by declaring that the Son of man had come to serve, and to give his life as a ransom for many' *(Mk 10:45 Mt 20:28)*. The climax of the service is the sacrifice. The Son of man is he who is aware of his dignity as Son of God: and far from having himself served by others, he wants to serve, 'and in the sacrifice he places himself completely at the disposal of all, since his life is given as a ransom for humanity.

But, as well as that, the service of the washing of the feet was done in anticipation of the sharing of the paschal meal. Because of this, it is seen as being linked to the mystery of the Eucharist. It shows the meaning of what is going to be new about this paschal meal. The climax of the service at table, a height which had never before been reached and which would never again be attained by anyone, was that the One who served gave himself as food and drink. It was a service possible only for One who was God. He served to the point of placing himself at the complete disposal of the guests' hunger and thirst. In his humility, he went so far as to have himself accepted as food and drink.

From then on, the Eucharist has contained within itself the power of humble love which led to the washing of the feet. The command to wash one another's feet would be stamped on the behaviour of the disciples if they sought, in the eucharistic meal, the humility which would enable them to put themselves in the last place instead of claiming the first, and to serve to the end. Those who receive the body of the Lord and who open themselves to its spiritual influence, are transformed by it in such a way that they adopt the attitude of service and humble devotedness that inspired the institution of the Eucharist. This attitude enables them to avoid quarrels or to go beyond those which may arise, by renouncing all the pretensions of self-love.

2. The kingdom of love

It was within the framework of the eucharistic meal that Jesus announced the new commandment. With the newness of the Eucharist came the newness of the moral conduct which, from then on, would characterise Christians.

In fact, Jewish law prescribed love of one's neighbour. In response to the scribe who had asked him what was the first commandment, Jesus had replied by citing the precept of the love of God as it was formulated in the law, and then love for others: 'You shall love your neighbour as yourself' *(Mk 12:31)*. He limited himself to repeating the words used in the book of Leviticus (Lev 19:18). Therefore he considered that this text had kept its value. To love one's neighbour as oneself meant acting towards others as one wished to be treated oneself. On another occasion, Jesus commented on this rule by drawing attention to its capital importance: 'So whatever you wish that men would do to you, do so to them; for this is the law and the prophets' *(Mt 7:12)*.

While fully accepting this precept of the law, he showed that he gave it the widest meaning possible. Through the parable of the good Samaritan, he got the scribe to understand that 'the neighbour' to be loved could not be understood in a limited or restrictive way, and that in fact each one should become the neighbour of everyone else. In particular, traditional enemies like the Samaritans could not be regarded as strangers to the obligation decreed by the law. In speaking about the generous behaviour of a Samaritan towards a Jew, he wanted to overturn the prejudices which impeded friendly relationships between the Samaritans and the Jews.

This unlimited widening of the law was already something new which broke down the very narrow frontiers imposed on love. On this fundamental point of his doctrine, Jesus did not want to limit himself to a more open interpretation of ancient prescriptions. The Master had shown his express desire to correct the teachings of Jewish tradition. On the subject of the demands made by loving others, he said several times; 'You have heard that it was said ... but I say ...' *(Mt 5:21-46)*.

He opposed everything which could encourage hatred of one's enemies with the bold precept; 'Love your enemies and pray for those who persecute you'. This boldness was founded on the example of the Father who shows his favour to all, both those who are hostile to him and those who try to please him (Mt 5:44-45). No less bold was the precept of turning your other cheek to the one who strikes you (Mt 5:39). It was a command to struggle against violence by using gentleness.

This desire to substitute old prescriptions with new ones was revealed in all its breadth when Jesus gave the new general commandment of love. He chose the eucharistic meal, when his disciples were united to him in a spirit of intimate communion, to declare: 'Love one another as I have loved you' *(Jn 13:34; 15:12)*. He insisted on the fact that it was his own commandment, 'My commandment', the one which was and is so much his own that it was the sign by which his disciples would be recognised (Jn 13:35). This commandment was 'new'. The Master, this time, no longer contented himself with echoing the ancient law.

Where exactly is the newness to be found? It is found in the model assigned henceforth to mutual love from that time on: 'As I have loved you.' Jesus was alluding to the love to which he would bear witness in his painful offering.

But he was thinking, at the same time, of the love shown by the institution of the Eucharist. That is what John's Gospel suggests, because it begins the account of the Last Supper with the statement: 'Having loved his own who were in the world, he loved them to the end' *(Jn 13:1)*. He seemed to want to express the most extreme love which would be unfolded in the Eucharist. We have noted how the love went to the end, in the fact that, as well as the commitment to sacrifice, it included the commitment to the continual gift of himself for the future.

From then on, it was the love involved in the Eucharist which would constitute the model of the charity required of Christians. Now the Eucharist does not only present the highest model of love. It also communicates the strength to imitate this love. It could seem impossible to observe the precept which Jesus announced. How could the disciples love one another the way the Lord, in person, loved them? The problem was solved by the eucharistic meal. A higher energy, which enables Christians to love one another to the end, enters into them with the body and blood of Christ. With the solid food which affirms their will to love, they receive an inebriation which develops their enthusiasm in love.

In fact, the words, 'as I have loved you', do not just give an example to be followed. They signify a principle of life from which love results. Through the Eucharist, the love of Christ comes to take over the hearts of Christians in order to commit them more resolutely on the way of charity.

3. The most perfect unity

We have pointed out how the problem of unity was posed from the beginning of the meal because of the disciples' quarrel. Jesus had responded to it by an action which taught the attitude essential for preventing and settling quarrels, the most humble service. He did not stop there. His aim was not simply to get his disciples to understand well on a human level, a renunciation of the pretensions of human love. He wanted to propose a much higher ideal of unity which was in conformity with the precept of mutual love which he left them. He daringly placed this precept on a divine level by giving his own love, as the Son of God made man, as the model and source. He did the same with unity. He gave it a divine foundation and dimensions.

He had already revealed his own identity as Son by emphasising his total union with the Father. All the works which he accomplished showed that he had received everything from the Father. That is why nobody could take the sheep which belonged to the Good Shepherd out of his hand. It was even more impossible to take anything out of the Father's hand. Christ's hand and the Father's hand were indissolubly bound to each other. Jesus also said 'The Father and I are one' *(Jn 10:30)*.

This is the unity which should be the principle of union among believers. In the priestly prayer, the plea for unity is based on the repeated declarations about the wonderful union between the Father and the Son: 'That they all may be one; even as thou, Father, art in me, and I in thee, that they also may be one in us, so that the world may believe that thou hast sent me. The glory which thou hast given me I have given to them, that they may be one even as we are one, I in them and thou in me, that they may become perfectly one, so that the world may know that thou hast sent me and hast loved them even as thou hast loved me' *(Jn 17:21-23)*.

Jesus wanted to ensure perfection in unity. When he was formulating his precepts concerning charity, he had made a general statement; 'You, therefore, must be perfect, as your heavenly Father is perfect' *(Mt 5:48)*. Thus he gave the highest model possible for striving for perfection. He had applied it in a more particular way to love of enemies, which should enable his disciples to behave as sons of the heavenly Father, whose sun and rain are given to all, friends and enemies (Mt 5:45). Charity consists in loving the way the Father does, just as it consists in loving the way Christ does, since the Father and the Son are inseparable in unity.

When it came to proposing a model for unity among Christians, we can understand why Jesus highlighted the unity of the Father and the Son. It is only in this light that the real objective of his work could be properly understood — the creation of a human community in the image of the divine community. It is only in seeing this reflection of the divine unity in human unity, that we can discover the origin and mission of Jesus: 'that the world may believe that thou hast sent me'. There is a call to faith in the witness of a unity which goes beyond human possibilities.

We can imagine that this unity must have been a profound aspiration of the Master's eucharistic heart. How many times must Jesus' heart have been torn by his disciples' quarrels! He waited impatiently for the moment when not only could he place an ideal of perfect unity before them and pray to the Father to make it a reality in them, but when he could give them the strength to strive towards this unity. From now on, he was able to communicate this strength to them directly through the Eucharist and to supply the source of it to them for the future.

It is true that we could wonder what relationship there is between the Eucharist and the model given of the unity of the Father and the Son. The Eucharist is the sacrament in which Christ hands himself over as a personal presence. It has a direct christological dimension rather than a trinitarian one. It is only the Son of God who gives himself as food and drink in the eucharistic meal. The eucharistic sacrifice is also proper to the Son. It is the Son who offers himself to the Father in the Holy Spirit and he is the only one who offers himself.

However, we cannot forget that when he presented the Eucharist, after the multiplication of the loaves, Jesus had insisted on the primordial role of the Father in the eucharistic meal. It is the Father, in effect, who gives us our daily bread. It is he who gives the real bread from heaven (Jn 6:32). Jesus said that the food which remains for eternal life is given by the Son of man, but that, at the same time, it is given by the Father (Jn 6:37). So the Eucharist shows the unity of the Father and the Son in a special way. It is this unity that is the model of union among Christians which they receive through the eucharistic meal. It brings a constant principle of union and coming together to the depths of human hearts, which tend so much to be divided. It brings about, in an ever fuller way, the unity which Christ implored for his Church.

4.   Peace

The gift of peace appertains to the gift of unity. Just as the disciples' quarrels endangered the future of the Church, they also threatened the inner peace necessary to its development.

It was in the widest sense possible that Jesus said to his disciples; 'Peace I leave with you; my peace I give to you; not as the world gives do I give to you' *(Jn 14:27)*. The comparison made with the peace given by the world shows that it is an external peace established by harmonious relationships between people. The world wants to achieve this but cannot do so. We sense in the words of the Master an allusion to the numerous disappointments which human history provides for those who seek peace.

Jesus gives his peace differently, in other conditions. He does not give it in a fragile or unstable way, which would be the constant cause of fears of conflict or rupture. He ensures a profound and lasting peace, because it does not consist only in external agreement, but in an understanding inscribed in the depths of the soul. It is his peace which he gives, a peace which he bears within himself and which he communicates to humanity by placing it within people's hearts.

What precisely is this gift of peace? Jesus did not explain, but we must remember that Paul calls him 'our peace', because he had reconciled all people with God and among themselves. This reconciliation implies that relationships of hostility and hatred disappear. It is so total that, in Christ, all humanity constitutes 'one new man' *(Eph 2:14-16)*.

So Christ established peace first of all in each human person's relationship with God, by obtaining the remission of each one's sins. It is essentially sin which disturbs peace. Firstly, it causes the most radical conflicts, because it concerns the creature's position before the creator and tries unsuccessfully to break our bonds of dependence with the divine sovereignty. When sinners are in conflict with themselves, with their consciences, they are, in reality, in conflict with God, because the voice which speaks in the depths of our conscience is the divine voice of the Holy Spirit. Secondly, it arouses remorse and profound uneasiness, because of the deep contradiction between what people should be, and what they are. Only the forgiveness of sins can bring an effective remedy to this situation which would otherwise be hopeless. Inner contradiction disappears because of this pardon, human beings find harmony again with God and so accord with themselves and with their consciences.

Thanks to the inner peace which they receive they can form better relationships with others, following the principle that all reconciliation with God brings with it reconciliation with our neighbour. This principle belongs to the mystery of the work of salvation, but it also corresponds to a fact of human psychology. Those who enjoy deep peace within themselves are able to spread peace more easily. Their intimate harmony is reflected in their relationships with others.

We can see that Jesus, as he is presented to us in the gospels, is an example of this. He appears as a man of peace and wonderful serenity. His relationship with the Father was full of harmony at each moment and this harmony gave a peaceful tone to all that he did. He was certainly the object of much hostility and contradiction, but it was never he who aggravated the conflicts. He always tried to bring out the points of agreement which he found in his interrogators. He carried the peace of God within him and that is why he could say, 'my peace'.

He was the first to fulfil the ideal which he gave in the Beatitudes: 'Blessed are the peacemakers, for they shall be called sons of God' *(Mt 5:9)*. He was the Son of God in a unique sense and he was a peacemaker because of his union with the Father. There was perfect understanding between him and the Father and he wanted to share it.

When he gave this beatitude he showed the importance which he attached to the efforts to establish peace in social relationships. He did not achieve world peace, but he wanted to foster peace in the world and he wanted his disciples to become peace-makers, agents of peace.

In the Eucharist he gave the sacrifice which brings reconciliation between humanity and God, and also reconciliation among people. This sacrifice gives the most essential contribution to the work for peace. Through the eucharistic meal he gathers his faithful together in union and peace. The One who gives his flesh as food and who, according to Paul, is our peace, nourishes all the initiatives and undertakings for peace in all those who receive it. Since his blood is the blood of the covenant and, through it, he unites people among themselves, his Eucharist propagates everything which is covenant and agreement of wills. In all aspects of individual and social human life, the Eucharist helps a spirit of peace to reign with the serenity which was so characteristic of the gospel Jesus.

THE ASPIRATION FOR A CLIMATE OF CONFIDENCE AND JOY

1. The exhortation to confidence

During the dramatic circumstances in which the Last Supper took place, Jesus tried to encourage his disciples to be confident. He knew much better than they, the trial they were going to have to face. They did not realise the violence of the storm that was going to hurl itself at them. He wanted to prepare them for the great shock.

'Let not your hearts be troubled; believe in God, believe also in me' *(Jn 14:1)*. There was a remarkable daring in the exhortation. Jesus was asking them to have the same faith in him as the Jewish people had in God. The new faith was faith in his person. And it was this faith which, from then on, would be the rampart which would protect the disciples from the inner blows which would threaten them.

Of course, it was not a question of abandoning the ancient faith, but of confirming it with this new orientation. Faith in Jesus was faith in God, because he was revealed to humanity as God. Also, it was faith in the Son, a Son intimately united to the Father and inseparable from him. 'Believe me that I am in the Father, and the Father in me' *(Jn 14:11)*. Faith in the Son was, therefore, indissolubly bound up with faith in the Father. But it became the essential process of faith. It was no longer enough to believe in an invisible God. It was necessary to believe the Son of God made man, in the Son of man, as Jesus had asked of the man born blind whom he cured on the Sabbath: 'Do you believe in the Son of man?' *(Jn 9:35)*.

The faith which Christ asked for at the Last Supper was the result of all that had been revealed to his apostles. They had already professed their faith. But the Master asked them to keep up their faith throughout the painful events which they were soon going to face. He told Peter that he had prayed that his faith would not fail (Lk 22:32). The great problem is of keeping the faith in a terrible moment of crisis.

We cannot separate this faith from the eucharistic context. Jesus said 'Believe in me', during the meal when he gave his flesh to eat and his blood to drink. So the faith that he asked for was especially faith in the Eucharist. We must remember that when he first announced the Eucharist, he had insisted very strongly on the need for faith, so strongly that some modern commentators see a teaching on faith rather than on the Eucharist in the first part, or even in the whole of the discourse. We have noted that in fact it was always the Eucharist that was the object of the discourse, but seen from the angle of faith, because this is the faith that was in question for his listeners. It was understood even in words which do not mention the

Eucharist specifically, for example; 'For this is the will of my Father, that everyone who sees the Son and believes in him should have eternal life; and I will raise him up on the last day' *(Jn 6:40)*. Consequently the gift of eternal life and the guarantee of resurrection on the last day are for those who eat the flesh of the Son of man and drink his blood (Jn 6:54). To believe in the Son is to believe in his Eucharist.

So the Eucharist is a source of confidence in times of trial. Jesus asked those who took part in the first eucharistic meal to believe in the efficacy of the meal in which he gave himself as food and drink. It was by means of this meal that he enabled them to face the fast-approaching storm and to keep their peace of heart, in spite of the perturbation they were going to go through in their attachment to him and in their convictions. The Eucharist was especially suited to give them serenity, because it was meant to give his own dispositions of soul to his disciples.

In order to understand the Eucharist even better we must remember that it is a commitment to sacrifice and that it tried to get the disciples to share in the heroic generosity which animated the Saviour in his offering. As well as that, it was based on the glorious consummation of the sacrifice which was anticipated at the Last Supper, since the Christ who gave himself as food and drink was Christ in his glorious state, the Lord risen from the dead and ascended into heaven. It was this perspective which gave Jesus' words their full value: 'In the world you have tribulation; but be of good cheer, I have overcome the world' *(Jn 16:33)*.

Jesus did not say, 'I will overcome the world' but, 'I have overcome the world'. He anticipated the victory which the Eucharist implied. It was as the conqueror of the world that he gave himself in the eucharistic meal. Victory over the forces of evil at work in the world had already been won.

From then on, confidence, as well as optimism and hope, would flow from the Eucharist. It is stronger than all the evil which is loose in the universe. Every eucharistic sacrifice is more powerful than the sins of the world; it obtains pardon. Every eucharistic meal gives Christians the strength to conquer the power of evil in themselves and to remain faithful. It lets the Saviour's victory into their hearts.

2. The announcement of joy

In the eucharistic heart of Jesus, the aspiration to open the way of joy to his disciples was no less strong than his desire to support and develop their confidence. The final objective of his coming on earth as Saviour was to give the greatest possible happiness to humanity.

During the Last Supper the Master faced his disciples clearly with the suffering which they would undergo. He had announced that he himself would have to suffer greatly as part of the Father's plans. The same was true for his disciples; they would have to 'suffer greatly' because it was not light pains that were going to strike them. The great trial of the passion shows the immense weight of the cross which the disciples would have to carry. So Jesus did not leave his followers under any illusions about an easy or comfortable life.

But even though he placed his disciples' future within the context of the drama of redemption, Jesus insisted more on the joy which should result from the suffering. He never separated the announcement of the passion from the announcement of the resurrection. Each time that he declared that the Son of man must suffer and die, he added that he would rise again on the third day. During the Last Supper when he said to his disciples, 'A little while, and you will see me no more', he continued, 'again a little while, and you will see me' *(Jn 16:16)*. The sorrow which they felt during the drama of Calvary would be followed infallibly by the joy of seeing the Master alive again.

The announcement was mysterious and raised questions in the disciples' minds. In reply, Jesus did not give any other explanation about the events of the death and resurrection, because they could be understood only after they had taken place. But he made clear to the disciples what their own dispositions of soul should be in relation to these events. In contrast with the facile joy which reigns in the world, they would travel by a painful path which would lead them to a joy of the highest worth. With his full authority as Master of revelation, he declared: 'Truly, truly, I say to you, you will weep and lament, but the world will rejoice; you will be sorrowful, but your sorrow will turn to joy' *(Jn 16:20)*. Just as the suffering was inevitable, it was as certain that it would not last. It would be transformed into joy.

It must be noted that Jesus did not just say that joy would come after sadness. He announced that the sadness would be transformed into joy. The implication was that there was a hidden source of joy within the trial. So suffering can never be seen as pure suffering. It always contains the seed of joy.

The comparison of the woman giving birth to a child makes this clear: 'When a woman is in travail she has sorrow, because her hour has come; but when she is delivered of the child, she no longer remembers the anguish, for joy that a child is born into the world. So you will have sorrow now, but I will see you again, and your hearts will rejoice, and no one will take your joy from you' *(Jn 16: 21-22)*. Suffering is a source of joy because it gives birth. It engenders a new humanity. The building of a better world is paid for by sacrifice. Now this fruitfulness is such that it makes us forget the sharpness of the suffering and we appreciate fully the resulting joy.

The Eucharist committed the disciples very profoundly to the redemptive sacrifice. It gave them the strength to bear and offer the suffering, however heavy it might be. It involved them in the trial only to enable them to taste an equal joy.

The eucharistic sacrifice is a source of joy because it makes present the offering of Calvary and also the mysteries of the resurrection and ascension. The joy which joins Christians to the Saviour's triumph goes beyond all the pain caused by their offering in union with the cross of Christ.

The eucharistic meal is a source of joy because of the very nature of a meal which should cause euphoria, with the inebriation symbolised by the wine. Since the Christ who gives himself is the glorified Christ, he brings us into the heart of the joy which accompanies the resurrection. By sharing in this meal, Christians receive a special grace to lead their lives in sincere joy.

The eucharistic presence is a source of joy for those who welcome it and respond to the permanent gift of himself which the Lord makes. It calls us to contemplation and to experience the happiness that contemplation brings. It helps Christians to come out of themselves, their worries and their sufferings, by turning towards the person of Christ, who radiates peace and joy under the sacramental sign.

The whole Eucharist flows ceaselessly from the heart of Christ and from his aspiration to give the most authentic happiness to humanity.